Joy O. I. Spoczynska is a former head of biology in a girls' school, who now writes books, mainly on natural history and on cookery, self-sucficiency and related subjects. She has been able to put into practice at first hand many of the ideas she describes in this book. Her other published works include subjects as diverse as a history of the evolution of the fishes, an account of the social organization of the wasps, two petkeeping manuals for younger readers, a book on fossils, several books on field studies and a manual of self-sufficiency for the flat-dweller without a garden.

Joy O. I. Spoczynska

LOOK AFTER THE PENNIES

How to Save Money At Home

Line drawings by Kenneth H. Poole

Futura

For Jonathan
who once recycled a cycle into a moped, which is more
than I could do

Contents

Introduction

Home economy is not a new concept. It was the order of the day during World War II, when it went under the somewhat unromantic name of Make Do and Mend, alongside more inspiring campaigns such as Dig for Victory. Before this it was practised by the families of the unemployed during the years of the Depression following the 1914-1918 War. Still earlier, the poorer families of the Victorian era made it a way of life, despite the fact that the pound in those days had a vastly greater purchasing power than it does now.

To-day, unfortunately, we have rising unemployment – over three million according to present statistics – and life (and love) on the dole are once again a stark reality of life. Home economy is therefore coming into its own again. There are literally hundreds of ways in which savings can be made in all aspects of daily living – many of them ideas which will save not just pennies but pounds, often a good many pounds at one go, which will make an immediate impression on the budget as opposed to the smaller savings which mount up with time.

If, happily, you are in full employment, the same kind of home savings will enable you to save up sooner for that freezer, washing-machine or car that you've set your heart on – or the holiday in Florida for the whole family which you could never quite run to while the children were growing out of all their clothes faster than Jack's beanstalk.

A good many of the ideas in this book involve the re-using of good sound materials for new purposes. There are, when you come to think about it, very few materials that need be wasted. Paper, cloth, boxes, bottles, household cleaning product containers, jars, foil, cardboard, string, rubber, wood, tins, plastic yoghourt and margarine tubs, polystyrene supermarket trays – the list is endless. All these, and more, can be refashioned into something new after their initial use is over. Even big unwieldy old furniture can be rebuilt into modern space-saving units.

This is a book of *practical* ideas. I have not included any ideas which would cost more to put into practice than they are worth in terms of the end result. Most of the ideas have been tried and tested either by myself or by the various other people who have found them worthwhile enough to describe to me.

'A penny saved is a penny gained', runs the old saw – but most of these ideas will not save you just pennies but will leave you with pounds in the bank which can be put to some better use. As a bonus you will also have the feeling of satisfaction which comes when you have managed to make a really useful article from something which would otherwise have been a total loss.

This book tells you how.

J.O.I.S.

December 1983

Chapter One

The Kitchen: Food and Cooking

In the kitchen we use so many products of all kinds that the total number of times we use all the various items must run into thousands during the course of a year. It therefore follows that by taking a little thought it is possible to effect considerable savings in this area, on the principle that a large number of small savings will mount up during a period of time to a considerable sum.

There are two major operations that can save you a visible proportion of your expenditure at one go, so to speak. First of all, if you can grow most of your vegetables and some fruit, you can save up to one third of your entire food bill – more if you happen to be a vegetarian. This does, however, require that you have a garden or an allotment. You can, if you are flatbound, grow certain things in window-boxes, tubs, pots on the window-ledges and so on, but your scope is somewhat limited. Certain things just will not grow indoors and others need vast amounts of space (and soil) such as root vegetables. Within these limitations, you can still grow such things as lettuces, herbs, indoor cucumbers, etc. and thus make a valuable contribution to your budget. Don't forget that as well as cutting costs you are also ensuring that the vegetables you grow are free from poisonous chemicals and toxic sprays.

Just as an example, a packet of lettuce seed costs 19p at the time I write this, and contains approximately 500 seeds. A lettuce in the shops, or on the market stalls, costs from 12p (small) to around 20p (large round) or 25p for a cos or Webb's. Of course you definitely would need a garden to grow 500 plants, even allowing for succession sowing so that you did not have them all ready at the same time! But, assuming ownership of a garden, your saving in lettuces for the year could be anything up to £120 – and that's after I've made a generous allowance for the slugs!

The second operation that can save you pounds is shopping around. It may be more convenient to buy everything under one roof – that's what the owners of the big hypermarkets trade on. What their high-powered advertisements omit to mention is that it's not only more convenient to you, it's also more convenient to them, to the tune of several million pounds' annual profit! The 'loss leaders' attract you inside the store (10% off this, 8p off that, free gifts with something else) and once inside it's only human nature to say 'Oh, well, now that I'm here I might as well buy everything I need in this place – I'll be home a lot earlier than I will if I go and get the bus to Blogg's and another bus to the Whizzo Superstore and then another bus home!' Only by going to Blogg's and Whizzo do you discover that the difference between the prices you would have paid in the big hypermarket for the items that were not marked as loss leaders and those you pay in the two smaller supermarkets comes to a hefty £3.27 for the week's groceries. Multiply that by fifty (forget the two weeks' holiday) and you will have saved more than £150 over the year! (You can always write in to the transport authorities to complain about the recalcitrant buses.) And, inflation being what it is, you will be more likely to find that these price differences between shops increase rather than the reverse.

Just as an example from my own experience, the other day an identical-sized jar of my favourite coffee cost 35p more in one shop than in another, on the same day and in the same district! And in yet a third supermarket my normal brand of washing powder cost 23p more than in the shop where I had bought my supply! So, once again, I repeat: shop around. Allow yourself more time to enable you to do this; it will more than repay you in terms of financial savings, and be a real eye-opener into the bargain.

Another very important point that has a bearing on economy is the correct storage of the foods you purchase.

There is not much point in saving a sum equivalent to, say, one fifth of the housekeeping, if the items on which you made a saving are improperly stored and later have to be thrown into the waste bin because they have gone rotten! So ensure that you have a good fridge in working order and regularly defrosted (a fridge-freezer is even better) and well-ventilated larder shelves, bins, storage jars and so on for the non-perishables. Store any tins and jars in such a way that the ones purchased earliest are used first. It is helpful to date everything.

Now for all the money-saving tips I have promised you covering most of the goodies you are likely to use!

Save gas when cooking pasta
Bring a pan of water to the boil, throw in the spaghetti, noodles or other pasta, with salt if required, stir to prevent the pasta from sticking together and bring back to the boil. As soon as it has boiled turn off the gas, put a lid on the pan and leave it for twenty minutes, after which time it will be found to be perfectly cooked.

The over-salted stew
No need to panic! Chuck in a large raw (peeled) potato and leave it in for ten minutes while the stew continues cooking. The potato will absorb a good deal of the salt. Fish it out before serving.

Rescuing crystallized honey or jam
Stand the jar in a pan of hot water for as long as it takes (which is not usually very long) to liquidize the honey or melt the sugary crystallization of the jam.

Pick-me-up for a limp lettuce
No need to consign the weary-looking lettuce to the kids' rabbits. Just put it into a bowl of cold water with a few ice cubes and stand the bowl on the bottom shelf of the fridge. In half an hour it will have perked up.

A use for unwanted bacon rinds
Cut off the rinds from the raw bacon after purchase, put them into a plastic freezer bag and freeze. They may be cut into small pieces first. These are then used to flavour soups, stews, sauces, etc. and are also good in omelettes, quiches, etc. The rule is: when using them to flavour soups, stews and sauces use them uncooked; for use in omelettes and quiches, fry first until crisp before adding to the dish.

More juice from oranges and lemons
Roll oranges around on your worktop, pressing with your hand as you do so. This will make the orange produce much more juice. For lemons, drop them into a bowl of hot water and leave them for about ten minutes. This has the same effect. I don't know why these two methods do not seem to work the other way round!

Overcooked meat
So you forgot to turn off your oven after the joint was ready! Yes, it happens to everybody. The meat has now become tough and leathery – even the dog would not be able to get his teeth into it. *Nil desperandum*! Put it through the mincer and make a shepherd's pie. A nice crisp potato topping, some gravy and no one will recognize the burnt offering.

Overripe fruit
Cut off the bruised or discoloured soft parts and put the remainder into the liquidizer. This will make a good fruit sauce to serve with ice cream, blancmange, etc. A little sugar may be used to sweeten it if you are not too calorie-conscious.

Chicken economy makes sense
If you are going to roast or casserole a whole chicken, all well and good; but if you intend to cook a dish which uses separate chicken joints, why pay more than you need for ready-jointed legs, wings, etc. when it is much cheaper to

buy a whole chicken and joint it yourself? It is not at all difficult if you have a chopping-board and a *sharp* butcher knife or one of those 'mini' kitchen meat-choppers.

The basis of vegetable soup

Keep all left-over vegetables, cooked or uncooked, in plastic fridge containers, having first run them through the liquidizer. Label the containers with the contents, and when you need to make a vegetable soup choose the kinds most suitable for the recipe. These should not be kept too long before use (unless deep-frozen).

Stale cakes and biscuits for trifles

The sponge base of a trifle can be made from stale cakes and biscuits which, when soaked with sherry or fruit juice, are indistinguishable from fresh ones. If you are not contemplating making a trifle in the immediate future, freeze the cakes and biscuits until you are ready. They must be thawed out before use.

Overripe tomatoes can be saved

If they are not *too* far gone, leave them to soak in a bowl of salted cold water for thirty minutes, then rinse and wipe dry with a kitchen paper towel.

Eking out whipping cream

An egg white whisked to stiff peak stage, when folded into cream to be whipped, will make the cream go much further. However, this is not very satisfactory when the whipped cream has to be piped.

Make you own castor sugar

Ordinary white granulated sugar, which is much cheaper, can be ground into castor sugar in your liquidizer. The process takes only a few minutes.

How to revive stale bread

Dip the loaf in cold water or run it under the tap, and put it in the oven. The setting must be very low or you'll burn it. Leave it in the oven until it has dried, and you will find it restored to its original crispness. This can, of course, only be done with *uncut* loaves; if you put a sliced loaf in the oven it would become toast!

Saving on greasing cake tins
Butter and margarine wrappers, even lard and dripping wrappers, are just the job for greasing cake tins. No additional fat is necessary. Store them in a plastic bag in the bottom of the fridge until required. They will also be less messy to use if the fat has hardened.

An economy tip for jam-makers
When making jam, don't waste money buying transparent circles and waxed paper circles. These latter can be cut from the waxed paper in which cereals are packed inside their packets. Draw a circle round a jam-jar in each size you use, and cut several at a time using it as a pattern. The transparent circles can be cut from the transparent paper in which tights and stockings are packed. Save all your rubber bands, too. And, naturally, you save all empty jam-jars for re-use. Big ones, including pickle and coffee jars, are better for pickling, keeping the smaller ones for jams, lemon curd, marmalade, etc. Home jam and preserve making, pickling and bottling is time-consuming but will save you quite a lot of money, especially if you have a hungry family of children rushing home from school to fill up on jam butties until supper is ready!

If you use the fruits and berries of the hedgerow, the commons and the woods, you can make delicious jams for only the cost of the sugar and the gas for cooking.

Use wild plants as vegetables
Many wild plants can be used as vegetables. Dandelion and other leaves can be used in salads; fat hen, nettles, etc. can be cooked as spinach. Edible mushrooms abound and make tasty dishes, but you *must* know them! There are more then a hundred edible fungi, of which at least forty are very good. Get a good botany book from the public

library and learn to identify the best ones which grow in your area.

Leftover cheese for the fridge

Leave the cheese until hard, when it will be easier to grate. Keep the grated cheese in a sealed glass jar in the fridge until needed for adding to pasta dishes, sprinkling on soups, making sauces, using in omelettes, etc. If you run out of Parmesan it makes a very acceptable substitute and costs far less.

Basic white sauce cubes

By making these cubes you obviate the need to buy expensive ready-prepared sauce mixes. Mix together equal amounts of plain flour and butter. Fill an ice cube tray with the mixture and freeze. When you need to make a sauce, add one cube to a half pint of milk and heat slowly, stirring the while so that it does not burn, and add whatever flavourings and seasonings your recipe requires — salt, pepper, parsley, capers, or what not.

Another use for stale bread

Grate the bread into crumbs and store in the freezer until needed. It is a good idea to make two lots — one from hard bread (for use when coating fish, rissoles, etc.) and one from soft bread (for stuffings).

Two more uses for stale bread

Summer pudding, bread-and-butter pudding and similar puddings using bread as a basic ingredient are a tasty way of using those leftover stale loaves. Another use is to moisten the bread (cut off any crusts first) and squeeze it into ball shapes in the palm of the hand. Drop these into a stew about five minutes before the end of cooking time; they make terrific dumplings and save you all that kneading and mixing as well as the cost of suet, flour, etc. Do not cook them very long or they will disintegrate. The reason why regular suet dumplings require twenty minutes' cooking is because they are made from raw ingredients that have not been cooked.

Save gas or electricity when cooking

Instead of putting potatoes and two other veg. for boiling on to three different burners, wrap each vegetable, prepared, cut fairly small and seasoned, with a knob of butter on top, in a piece of kitchen foil, and boil these 'parcels' all together in one pot. They will not take any longer than if boiled separately.

Don't use the oven to cook only one dish. Fill the oven to make the most use of the heat. For example, if you are baking a meat pie, make two, bake both together and freeze one for use another day. Or you could put a meat pie in the middle of the oven and a fruit pie on the top shelf. You wouldn't want two pies at one meal, so the fruit pie can be put in the fridge after cooling and kept for tomorrow's meal. One point, though: when baking cakes do not bake anything else that needs looking at before the cake is ready, or it will sink in the middle when you open the oven door.

Gravy from vegetable water

Use some of the water in which vegetables have been cooked when making gravy. This saves on gas as the water is already hot, and the vitamins from the vegetables are much better in your gravy than going down the plug. If you have a lot of vegetable water – too much for just gravy – save it to make soup by adding various ingredients. If soup is not required immediately, freeze the vegetable water until you are ready to make it.

Saving electricity when cooking

Except when making soufflés or cakes, turn off the heat ten minutes before the end of cooking time. The oven or hob will retain enough heat to finish the cooking.

Another tip when boiling vegetables

Cut the vegetables into smaller pieces. They will then be cooked through in much less time.

Save gas when baking potatoes

When baking jacket potatoes, push a metal skewer right through the middle of each one lengthways. The metal acts as a conductor of heat and the potato will be cooked in half the time.

Two tips when buying bacon

Bacon is cheaper sold loose than when prepacked. You can also buy the exact quantity you need. When buying bacon to use in flans and quiches buy the much cheaper offcuts. The taste is just as good and they are much cheaper then rashers.

An idea for fish pies and fish cakes

Fish and chip shops often sell 'trimmings', which are odd pieces cut off the uncooked fish to make the fillets a convenient shape for frying. The fish will be a blend of cod, plaice, rock, etc. but no matter. Mixed in a fish pie they will taste fine. You can also use them for making fish cakes. The cost will be less than a quarter of the price of regular fish.

The joys of a triple saucepan

This is a saucepan which consists of three separate triangular-shaped pans fitting together to form the equivalent of one round pan. There is a handle (detachable) which fits all of them. Thus, three different items can be cooked at the same time on one ring. This is one of the most useful kitchen gadgets I have. Each of the three 'pans' has its own lid, too.

Double-cooking with a steamer

If you are going to steam a green vegetable such as cauliflower, why waste fuel by boiling plain water in the lower pan and cooking your potatoes separately? Cook the potatoes in the water below the steamer-top. If the steamed vegetable will be ready before the boiled potatoes, just take off the top while the potatoes finish boiling and replace it just before you are ready to dish up in order to reheat if cooled.

A tasty way to stretch home-made beefburgers
A half-pound of minced meat can be stretched to make as many burgers as a pound of the meat would do, if you combine it with the contents of one whole packet of sage and onion stuffing mix. Soak the mix first with cold water; it will fill out to more than twice its original bulk. Then combine it with the meat to make the burgers. Go easy on the salt and pepper – most packet mixes are well-seasoned already and it is unlikely you will need more than a dash of either. A beaten egg should be mixed in for binding. Turn out on to a floured board and shape into flattened rounds.

The four-way marrow-bone
Buy some marrow-bones for a few pence from your butcher. Simmer in water for three hours and leave to cool. Skim off the fat from the top and put into a freezer container to use later for roasting, etc.

Now make a tasty and nourishing soup by adding to the stock a few carrots, onions, leeks, turnips, parsnips or any other kind of vegetable you may have handy. Throw in a handful of pearl barley, add salt and pepper and cook. You can either serve 'as is' with the vegetables in chunky form, in which case don't overcook them until they are mushy and lose their appetising appearance; or you can bung the whole lot through the blender and then reheat with a little cream (do not boil or it will curdle) to produce a cream soup. Serve either kind with croûtons made from leftover stale bread. Then give the bones to the dog, who will bury them in the garden afterwards.

So, from a few pence worth of bones, you have a nourishing soup for the family, bones for the dog, fat for cooking, and – guess what? After the dog has buried the bones, they gradually become fertilizer for the garden – organic, too!

Gravy need never be wasted

Any gravy left over from your Sunday joint, with no prospect of being used next day with something else, can be frozen by pouring it into an ice-cube tray. When you need a stock cube, just use one of the frozen gravy cubes. Much more nutritious than bought stock cubes which are little more than compressed blocks of chemicals and synthetic flavourings. And, of course, you save by not buying the cubes.

A use for leftover mashed potato

Chop an onion very finely (or mince it) and blend with the mashed potato. Form into round flat cakes and sprinkle grated cheese on top. Cook in the oven, under the grill, or in the frying-pan. When the cheese is golden brown and bubbling, the potato cakes are ready.

Baking potatoes in the ashes

This is, of course, if you have an open fire. Scrub but do not peel some good-sized potatoes and wrap in kitchen foil. Put them in the ash pan under the fire and leave them for about two hours. Turn them over half-way through the cooking time. The fire must be going well to cook the potatoes in the above time. Remove when ready (test one with a fork) and eat with butter and salt.

Home-made potato crisps

Why pay exorbitant prices for bags of crisps when it is very easy to make them yourself? Make a good quantity at one time. Peel potatoes and slice them *thinly*. Cook for a few minutes in very hot fat until just golden, then remove immediately and drain off the fat (the easiest way to do this is to stand the chip-basket on a wad of kitchen paper towels spread out on a large plastic bag so that you do not get grease all over your worktop). When the crisps have cooled slightly, sprinkle with salt (don't overdo it) and then leave to cool completely before bagging them and storing them in the fridge. Save all your small plastic bags for this purpose, of course – the supermarkets do you a favour by giving you so many that you don't need to buy rolls of lunchbags!

A quick 'n' easy crumble topping
Grate shortbread biscuits over the cooked apples, rhubarb or whatever fruit you are using, and pop under the grill until golden-brown. This particular tip is not specifically a money-saver because you do have to buy the biscuits, but it does save a lot of time making the traditional crumble mixture. And it is said that time is money . . .

SOS – Save On Sugar
Add sugar to stewing fruit only when it is almost cooked, and you will find you need far less. Don't write and ask me why – I don't know!

Make your own breakfast cereal
Muesli can be made very easily at home and much more cheaply then buying it in health food shops. Mix coarse oatmeal with chopped dried fruits such as sultanas and raisins, chopped dates, chopped nuts (if liked), chopped apple (ditto), and a *little* Demerara sugar. Add milk, cream, yoghourt, orange juice or whatever you like.

A cheap ice cream substitute
Make up a thick custard, adding some vanilla essence and top of the milk (or cream) just before it has cooled, stirring in well, and freeze in small oblong fridge-containers; when turned out they will be 'bricks'.

Don't waste that sour milk
Leave it for a further couple of days in a warm place, then strain it through muslin (or a jelly-bag) overnight. The next day take the curd out of the muslin or bag and put into a bowl with salt, black pepper and chopped chives (or green spring onion tops). Blend well together. This makes a very tasty sandwich filling.

How half a pound of butter can become double

Bring half a pint of milk to the boil, remove from heat and allow to cool slightly. Cut half a pound of butter into small pieces and add to the milk, with a little salt. Now put it all into the blender and keep it going until it has thickened. Remove from blender and put into oblong butter dishes. It will solidify on cooling, and you will have two half-pound blocks instead of one. It also has the added advantage of staying smooth, soft and spreadable, even if kept in the bottom of the fridge.

A flour dredger for free!

Take an empty screw-top coffee jar and bore holes in the lid. Plastic lids are rather difficult to bore holes in, so try to find one which has a metal lid.

Optical illusions . . .

Don't forget that when the budget is tight some items can be made to appear greater in quantity by a number of artful dodges. Grate the cheese, shred the lettuce, chop the celery, and cut tomatoes in half and then each half into four wedges. Arrange things on smaller plates and the portions will look bigger!

None for the pot

Loose tea is much cheaper than teabags. Use one teaspoonful of tea per cup. The teapot will not be drinking any tea so it does *not* need the proverbial 'one for the pot'. After you have finished with the teapot, pour the dregs around your houseplants – cold tea seems to do them a power of good.

If you *must* use teabags, one will make *two* cups. Just fish it out and re-use. You may even like to dry them afterwards for re-use – it is amazing how many cups of tea you can make from one bag if the tea is of good quality. The cheaper ones will not stand up to such intensive use, though.

When defrosting the fridge
Save the water which accumulates on defrosting the fridge. This is distilled water, which has many uses such as topping up the battery in the car, using for steam irons, and diluting concentrated medicines. Store the distilled water in a sterilized carboy.

The answer is a lemon
When only a small amount of lemon juice is needed, pierce a hole in the lemon with a skewer (or stainless steel knitting needle) and squeeze out the amount you need. Then wrap the lemon in kitchen foil and store in the fridge until you need it again.

Rescuing stale buns
Dip the buns in milk and heat in a very low oven for a few minutes. Butter them while hot, and they will taste like fresh ones. Honestly!

Saving fuel when cooking
When at all possible, keep the lids on the pots and pans when cooking. The steam will stay inside the pan and help to cook the food in appreciably less time, instead of coming out and making the kitchen look like a Turkish bath. Grease-laden steam allowed to escape makes the windows very dirty and damages the surfaces of walls and ceilings.

Make your own icing sugar
This can be made for half the cost of buying it in the shops. Put it into the grinder attachment of your blender, and grind until the right consistency has been reached.

Succession cropping with mustard and cress
When buying mustard and cress in plastic containers, cut off the tops with scissors to use in your salad or whatever, then water the cut stalks and leave in a warm, shaded place. In eight to ten days a new crop will have grown. Two for the price of one! But why buy the ready-grown

article when you can grow it yourself? You do not even need soil. Just sprinkle the seeds on dampened kitchen paper towel or tissues, or even blotting paper, laid on the bottom of one of those polystyrene supermarket trays in which meat and similar items are packed. Water well, and keep in the dark until the seeds have germinated. Bring out into the light and the mustard and cress should be ready for cutting in about five to six days. The towelling must be kept damp, and once germinated the seedlings grow best in a shaded spot out of bright sunlight. This is indoor gardening at its simplest.

SOS – Save on Salt

Keep table salt for the table and use the much cheaper cooking salt for cooking. Block salt is cheaper still, but it needs to be ground first in a grinder, or grated if you have no food processor.

Recycle empty containers

Jam and pickle jars, plastic ice cream tubs, coffee jars, biscuit tins, yoghourt tubs, margarine tubs, etc. can all be recycled for use in the kitchen. Not many tins are suitable owing to small size, jagged edges, etc. (except biscuit tins which are useful for storing cakes), but most glass and plastic containers can be put to new uses. Large glass jars are particularly good for the storage of non-perishable goods such as lentils, rice, etc.

Tubs without lids can be used to start seeds (grow herbs on the kitchen window-ledge). Punch a few holes in the bottoms for drainage with a skewer or metal knitting needle made red-hot at one end over a flame. Be sure to hold the other end of the metal object with a pot-holder or something, since metal conducts heat very quickly and you could burn your hand badly if you are careless.

The aluminium foil dishes in which Chinese takeouts and some supermarket products are packed make ideal freezer containers. A sheet of kitchen foil makes the lid.

Cardboard containers may be cut up into convenient sizes for using as shopping-lists on the unprinted reverse side.

Kitchen paper towels as napkins
Kitchen paper towels make excellent table napkins for ordinary everyday family use, at a considerable saving in cost. Keep your 'proper' paper napkins for special occasions only.

Vinegar from pickles
When you have finished the jar of pickled onions or other clear pickles, save the vinegar and, blended with a little olive oil and seasoning, re-bottle it as vinaigrette salad dressing.

Make your own wines
Home winemaking is much easier than it looks. Borrow books on the subject from the public library. I make all my wines from hedgerow and woodland fruits and blossoms. All I pay for is the sugar and the yeast, and the wine works out at about 4p a glass.

Render unto freezer . . .
Render down all the excess fat from joints and poultry and keep in the freezer to use for roasting potatoes, frying and so on. Keep each kind in a separate container. Once the fat has cooled it can be poured into plastic containers, where it will solidify; but do not pour it in while hot, or the containers will buckle.

Tenderizing ox liver
Ox liver is, as you doubtless know, much cheaper than lamb's or pig's liver, but can be very tough and rather strong-tasting. If you cut it into very thin slices and let it lie in a dish of milk for about an hour, it will be very tender when cooked, and much milder in flavour.

Make 'sour cream' at home

Add a few drops of lemon juice to regular cream to make the kind of 'sour cream' sold at a more expensive price, if this is required in the recipe you are using.

Make your own bread

I'm not going to pretend that the first time you try baking your own bread it's going to come out perfect. It's easy once you're used to it, but it does take a bit of getting into.

The very first time I tried, the bread came out of the oven as hard as a slab of Jurassic rock. My ex-husband, who was a carpenter, could not even saw a slice off. In desperation we put it out for the birds, but they could not even peck an impression on it. It would have made a good door stop but we did not need one, so finally we went out and abandoned it in a remote spot, hoping that it would eventually biodegrade and become part of the environment. Frankly, I think it more likely that someone handed it in to a museum as an Iron Age relic.

I asked a home breadmaker whose offerings are always fantastic what she thought I had done wrong. She asked me where I obtained the yeast I had used, and I told her I had brought it with me from Crewe when I moved seven years ago.

'That's it!' she cried. 'The yeast must be *fresh*!' And that, it seems, is the secret! *Always* use *fresh* yeast each time.

Recipes are legion. A book in most public libraries, called *The Tassajara Bread Book*, gives nearly a hundred different recipes. I recommend it.

If you don't want to fiddle with yeast, kneading, proving, hanging about until the dough is ready and all the other things that go to make up the mystique of breadmaking, make unleavened breads such as chapatis. These can be knocked up in ten minutes flat and simply cannot go wrong. I consider them just as good as regular bread used to make sandwiches or as bread and butter with jam, honey or marmalade, and what is more, they are delicious used in this way, hot. The Gujarati purists may howl, but I stick to my guns! They are much more filling than regular bread, so you need less. As well as saving time you also save on flour, and you do not need any yeast. They are very economical on fuel as you cook them on top of the stove and do not need to use the oven.

They can also be rolled up like pancakes and filled with various savoury mixtures such as cooked vegetables or meat with herbs, onions or garlic. And if your budget really is at rock bottom, just dip them in gravy. Delicious!

Buying fruit and vegetables for half-price or less
Rush out to the market about half an hour before they start packing up their stalls for the night on weekdays, and particularly on Saturday-nights for the weekend. Most stallholders will be only too glad to sell you perishable fruit and vegetables at rock bottom prices to get rid of them and avoid having them hanging about and possibly going rotten on them and thus becoming a total loss. Occasionally, if you get there five minutes before they go, they will even give you a few items free. It pays to be adroit!

Under the stall . . .
The potatoes, onions, etc, that roll under the stall can usually be picked up free. After all, you would have to wash or peel them first before cooking anyway. If you're short of money, this is no time to be fussy. No one is going to stand and look at you – other last-minute shoppers are far too busy with their frenzied hunt for bargains.

Sometimes stallholders put out whole cases of perishables for collection with the rubbish, just because one or two of the items are bruised, split or whatever. Casting a selective eye over these may tide you over a financial rough patch.

Don't knock the humble potato
I wonder how many of you remember seven-for-six potatoes? Translated into plain English, these are potatoes sold

at seven pounds for six-pence, which was the price light-years ago! This price was in effect a penny per pound with one pound thrown in as a quantity bonus.

As at the time of writing this, potatoes are now 14p per pound – fourteen times their old price – and no quantity bonus either. Still, when you think about it, the potato is a most versatile vegetable: it can be boiled, mashed, fried, roasted, sautéed, chipped, steamed, etc. so it can be served in a different way every day of the week. A pound of potatoes, peeled thinly, will make enough chips to serve six portions of eggs, sausages, bacon or whatever and chips, or enough mash to accompany a family main meal. Creamed with butter and milk, mash can be transformed into a most delicious vegetable. Then you can bake potatoes in the oven and serve with butter, herbs, various savoury stuffings, minced meat, cheese, sour cream, etc., thus making a meal in themselves.

So don't knock the potato – your 14p is still an economical investment!

Make your own yoghourt

Bring a pint of milk just to the boil but do not let it actually boil. This process used to be known as 'scalding' milk, although lately I do not seem to see this term used in cookery books. Let it cool until it is just warm on the inside of your wrist – testing it as you would the milk from a baby's bottle.

Take a carton of commercial plain yoghourt at room temperature (not straight from the fridge), and take from this a large heaping tablespoon of the yoghourt. Mix it in a bowl with the milk, and cover with a warmed tea-towel. Stand the covered bowl in an airing cupboard, over a boiler or hot pipes, or similar warm situation, and leave *undisturbed* for about eight hours – overnight is OK so long as the boiler or pipes are not turned off!

By the end of that time the milk will have become yoghourt. Put into plastic tubs and chill in the fridge. One such tub will contain the 'starter' for your next batch. After about five or six uses of home-made yoghourt starter, you will need to introduce a fresh culture by using commercial yoghourt again.

Flavourings can be added if required, using sugar (or artificial sweetener), chocolate, cocoa, coffee, fruit, honey, molasses, etc. These should be introduced *after* the yoghourt proper has been made, as in some cases the ingredients used may interfere with the action of the yoghourt-producing bacteria. Try to avoid too much stirring of the flavourings into the basic yoghourt, or it may become too sloppy. A good way of ensuring that the eventual fruit yoghourt will be 'set' is to add fresh fruit to the yoghourt and eat them together. You may find that the 'set' will vary among different batches; this may be due to the temperature, or to the degree of vitality of the live yoghourt bacteria. The main essentials are to ensure that the temperature does not fluctuate during the maturing period, and that the bowl is not moved or otherwise disturbed.

Thus, from one pint of milk and one 5oz tub of commercial plain yoghourt, you will be able to make approximately eight tubs of yoghourt, at about one third the price you would have had to pay in the shops.

Chapter Two

The Kitchen: Laundry and Cleaning

Our grandmothers certainly knew a thing or two when it came to washing and cleaning. They didn't have any aerosol sprays, biological detergents, washing machines, spin-dryers, tumble-dryers, silicone cloths, nylon brushes and all the other paraphernalia which we try to convince ourselves that we cannot do without. They managed with good old-fashioned hot water and soap, soda, household ammonia and the old-time equivalent of our modern Vim, which I seem to remember was called Glitto. For optical whitener in the wash they used a blue bag. They squeezed the water out of the washing through a mangle and had lots and lots of snow-white sheets (all washed by hand) billowing in the breeze from the wooden dolly-pegs on the clothesline. Above all, they used lashings of a commodity known as elbow grease. They found a certain grim satisfaction, too, in all this honest sweat and toil.

Water had to be boiled in heavy copper kettles, and before the advent of gas and electricity a fire had to be built first. In the more rural areas there was a wash-house with a copper which was laboriously filled with water from buckets, and a fire built underneath.

Our grandmothers did not even have a Hoover but had to go down on their hands and knees with a brush and pan to remove dust from carpets and rugs, and from time to time take them up and hang them over the clothes-line in the garden, where they would be vigorously beaten with a paddle-like instrument of cane called a carpet-beater.

Then there was the grim chore of blackleading grates and black range stoves – the most hated task in the household . . .

All this drudgery we can well do without, and thank our lucky stars that modern methods have rendered most of these things obsolete. But one thing sticks out a mile: these women got their good results using only a few cleaning products. They did not need a different product for each operation. We can take a leaf – in fact several leaves – out of their book. And, naturally, this is going to save us quite a bit of money if about a third of our housekeeping will not be squandered on unnecessary items.

I think you can manage with: detergent washing powder, bleach, soap, household ammonia, washing-up liquid, Vim, lavatory cleanser and a good beeswax-based furniture polish. If you have any solid teak or mahogany furniture, or priceless antiques, Stephenson's 'Old English' white furniture cream is better than solid furniture polish. It does smell of turps rather than lavender, but this soon goes.

You don't waste money buying floor cloths, cleaning swabs and polishing-pad stockinette rolls, do you? Just think how you can re-use your old worn-out vests, pants, stockings and tights. The latter make splendid polishing-pads, rolled up into a ball, while the heavy cotton items such as old vests and pants, cut into suitable-size pieces, make terrific absorbent floor cloths, cleaning swabs, and damp cloths for wiping formica worktops, ledges and woodwork, painted surfaces such as doors to remove grubby finger-marks, and so on.

This now leaves you only a few small necessities to purchase such as good old-fashioned yellow dusters, a 'shammy' for the windows, a washing-up brush and a pan-scouring block.

Now we've disposed of the basics, I'll now go on to the money-saving tips and dodges which will make the pounds simply roll off your budget!

Stopped-up sinks, blocked pipes
Don't call Dyno-Rod and land yourself with a fat bill. First of all, chuck a handful of washing soda over the outlet and then pour boiling water down the pipe. If this does not dislodge the obstruction, repeat the process. In

obstinate cases, several repeated applications will usually disperse the blockage. Failing this, use one of those rubber plungers shaped like a bell. Only if this does not work either is the obstruction obviously more serious and a plumber must be called in.

Lengthen the life of candles
You *do* keep a few candles in your store cupboard in case of power cuts, don't you? Keep them in the fridge for a day or two before storing them. This hardens them so that they burn longer.

A new cover for the ironing-board
The legs of old pyjama trousers make excellent ironing-board covers, especially if they are made of thick flannelette.

Saving soap
Put all your too-small-to-use ends of soap into a plastic tub, and pour a little boiling water in each time, When the tub is full, it will have set into a cylindrical cake of soap. Peel off the plastic casing and use like any other soap. Soap jelly can be made by keeping the soap ends in a screw top jar and adding a large proportion of boiling water. Agitate vigorously until the soap has dissolved into the water. This soap jelly is most useful on washing-day.

It's cheaper to buy one large bar of soap rather than two small ones. If it's a bit big to handle, remember that it will soon become smaller as it's used!

If perfumed toilet soap is unwrapped and stored 'naked' in a drawer of clothing, it will not only perfume the clothing but harden and so last much longer. The only thing to remember is not to put a tablet of Devonshire Violets soap among your husband's shirts.

Old towels into face flannels
When a towel becomes thin and worn, cut out the remaining good parts and hem the edges, and you have face flannels.

Cleaning the fridge

After defrosting the fridge, wipe all the surfaces with a cloth wrung out in warm water in which bicarbonate of soda has been dissolved. It not only cleans but deodorizes the fridge. Fridge deodorant blocks are a waste of money.

Sharpening scissors

Cut a piece of sandpaper or emery cloth several times with the scissors. This sharpens them.

Dog biscuits from stale bread ends

If you have a dog, save the crust ends from loaves, cut them into four squares by cutting in half and then again at right angles, and bake until really hard. This should, of course, be done at the same time that you are baking cakes or pies. Lay them at the bottom of the oven. What has this to do with cleaning, you may ask? Simply that when you are cleaning out the kitchen you are more likely to come across those stale bread ends . . .

Sharpening a sewing-machine needle

The same method can be used as that for sharpening scissors. Just 'sew' a piece of sandpaper, but without the thread. A few times will suffice.

Squeezy sponge mops

Pop a plastic bag over the head of the mop after each use. This will prevent its drying out and cracking, and add months to the life of the sponge.

A use for worn-out rubber gloves

Cut the fingers into small rubber-bands and the hand part into large ones. The fingers can also be used as finger-stalls. Cut off those that are not damaged and keep them in the first-aid box. You *do* have a first-aid box, don't you? Every home should have two, not one. One is kept in the kitchen where it will be most useful; another larger 'stock' box is kept in the bathroom. Any first-aid book will give a list of the items you should keep in the boxes. If you have a car, you should keep yet a third box in your glove compartment. Even if you don't need first-aid while driving your car, you may see someone else on the road who does.

The ubiquitous clothes-peg
Spring-clip pegs are useful for lots of other things besides hanging out your wash. They will secure open grocery packets or bags, close fridge and freezer bags, clip together shopping lists, bills, money-off coupons cut from papers and magazines, etc.

Hanging up brooms, brushes, etc.
Ring-pulls from beer and soft drink cans can be nailed to the handles of cleaning tools such as brooms and brushes, which can then be hung up on the wall out of the way. If you store these items in a broom cupboard, the floor space saved will then accommodate your vacuum cleaner, pair of steps, or some similar item.

Dispersing kitchen odours
Strong food odours left on wooden chopping boards, such as those from onions or garlic, may be dispelled by applying a paste made of bicarbonate of soda and water. Leave for a short time and then scrub thoroughly, afterwards rinsing under the cold tap.

A teaspoonful of mustard powder added to the washing-up water will remove the smell of fish from cutlery, and a teaspoonful of vinegar in the water will remove it from china. If a fishy smell lingers in a cooking pot, boil vinegar and water in it.

A musty smell in a vacuum flask which has not been used for some time can be dispersed by putting two teaspoons of bicarbonate of soda into the flask and topping up with boiling water. Leave overnight, then rinse several times with plain warm water after emptying. A lump of sugar in a dry flask will help to keep it fresh during storage.

Grease spots on wallpaper
These can be removed by holding a piece of blotting paper over the greasy mark and ironing over it with a warm iron.

Emulsion paint blobs on the carpet
If you are as ham-handed as I am at painting and decorating (although I am a dab hand at wallpapering) you will end up with emulsion blobs on the carpet sure as eggs is eggs. Yes, I *know* you spread a layer of newspapers, cloths or plastic rubbish-bags on the floor first, but I'm sure you also know (or will find out soon enough) that emulsion paint goes right through newspaper and cloth, and slides off the edges of plastic bags, so you'll most likely still have some blobs, though not so many as if you didn't use the protecting layers.

Let it dry first, then rub with a clean cloth soaked in meths. This is much cheaper than using turps.

If you don't mind reeking of meths for a bit, the stuff will also remove emulsion paint from your hair, hands and face, and clothes. I don't recommend you to use it on the dog. Put up with a spotted dog instead. If she's a bitch, rename her Madge (short for Magicote).

The DIY buffs say that you should avoid blobs in the first place by not filling your brush so full – the unmistakable mark of the amateur.

Got some gum, chum . . .
. . . in the wrong place? On the carpet or rug? Or anywhere else it should not be? Press an ice cube firmly on the gum and it will become brittle and crack easily, when it can be removed by scraping.

Window magic
More nonsense has been written about methods of cleaning windows than almost any other aspect of house cleaning. Meths, vinegar, newspaper, glycerine, plain water, washing-up liquid – you name it and it's almost sure to have been put forward as a viable alternative to expensive proprietary cleaners. Even paraffin was sugges-

ted in one magazine article! Another one suggested ammonia.

Do as I do and use the old-fashioned thick pink liquid of which Windolene is an example. Supermarkets' own brands of the same type of liquid are considerably cheaper and just as good. A large bottle will last for ages. All you do is put some on a damp 'shammy' and *leave it to dry on the surface*; that is the whole secret of sparkling windows! Then rub off with one duster and finally polish the glass with another clean duster. Unlike many of the products mentioned above, this one leaves no pong.

Grubby telephone receivers
Wipe the telephone over with a rag dampened with meths and all greasy, grubby marks will disappear.

Shining chromium plating
Bicarbonate of soda is as good as anything to put a shine on chrome taps and other fittings. Put it on with a damp rag and then buff vigorously.

Keeping the silver bright
Table silver can be kept bright by using a home-made polishing cloth which you make by mixing one tablespoon of ammonia and one teaspoon of plate powder and 6 fl oz of water. Soak a cloth in this mixture and hang it out to dry without squeezing any of the moisture out. It can be kept in a jam-jar or plastic tub on the kitchen sink-top. After the silver has been washed up and dried, it is then polished with the cloth.

Removing stains from flower vases
This is easy. Just fill the vase with a 1-in-4 solution of bleach and water, and in a few minutes all stains will have disappeared. Rinse thoroughly before using again for flowers. The same treatment will get rid of tea and coffee stains from cups, jugs and china teapots.

Washing-up liquid economy

Buy supermarkets' own brands, or Boots' own brand, in the largest size possible, and decant into smaller containers half- filled with water. The 50-50 diluted washing-up liquid is just as effective as the full strength normally used.

Brillo pad economy

Cut each pad in half and the pad will last twice as long. Wrap in kitchen foil after use and it will not go rusty.

Washing powder economy

Bore a small hole only instead of tearing back the entire flap. Then 'case' the packet in a plastic bag which fits round it closely, to avoid the packet disintegrating from standing on a wet surface or being splashed with hot water.

A good tablespoonful of bicarbonate of soda added to the washing water will soften the water, loosen stubborn grime and also cut down the amount of washing powder you need to use. I couldn't believe it the first time I tried it! Try it and see for yourself.

Automatic-type washing powder, which is cheaper than the ordinary kind, may be used equally effectively in non-automatic washing machines. It is not so good for hand-washing, though.

Drying the wash outdoors

Fold sheets in four and peg to the line with three pegs along one fold. The materials will not then drop out of shape, and will therefore be much easier to iron.

Choose a windy day when hanging out a candlewick bedspread. Peg it with the fluffy pile inside, and the friction caused by the wind will bring it up beautifully.

When drying woollen garments on a line, thread a nylon stocking through the sleeves and peg this to the line. You will not then have unsightly peg marks on the garment. Woollen garments are best laid on an absorbent towel on a flat surface to dry, however, as they are liable to stretch bigger when hung up.

Uses for soapy water after doing the washing

Used washing water can be recycled to save on soaps and detergents. It can be used to clean the sink, the bathroom wash-basin and the loo, and for swabbing tiled surfaces in the kitchen and bathroom. If you still have some left after this, use it for washing floors.

Whiter than white

A squeezed-out lemon skin dropped into the water when boiling whites will bring them up cleaner and whiter then you would have thought possible. They will smell fresh, too. White nylon garments should always be washed separately from coloured items; nothing makes them gradually turn a dingy grey faster than washing them all together. The blue bag, too, is useful if you have a lot of white goods to be laundered.

If you live in a heavily-polluted industrial district, be sure to wipe your clothes-line before use. Nothing is more infuriating when taking your washing down from the line than to find whites smudged with sooty marks.

Dashing away with the smoothing iron

Fold large items such as sheets into more or less the same folds that they will have when put away, and iron smaller items such as handkerchieves on top. You will then find that the uppermost side of the large item is ironed. Turn it to the opposite side and repeat the procedure. Then turn it inside out and iron another item, and so on until the whole sheet or other large item is smooth and ready to put away. You save not only time and effort but heat.

Measure your washing powder

Keep a measuring container such as a plastic yoghourt tub by the sink when washing. It's easy to pour too much detergent into the wash, but this is wasteful and your clothes will be no cleaner.

A sprinkler for ironing

Rinse out an empty spray-nozzle squeezy bottle such as

the plastic containers which hold washing-up liquid. The top will come off if you lever the edge with a small screwdriver. Filled with water, this will make a sprinkler for ironing.

Saving on heat when ironing
Leave till last the easy-care or so-called 'non-iron' items (which are almost always improved by a light ironing). Switch off the electricity after you have done all the other items. The cooling of an electric iron is a slow process and enough heat will remain to do the light smoothing of the easy-care items.

Saving when washing up
Don't use the sink, or a huge washing-up bowl, to do the dishes. If you use only a small bowl you will save on both hot water and washing up liquid.

You can save on washing up liquid in two ways. When a bottle is half-empty, fill it up to the top with water. When you buy a new one pour half into a jar and do the same thing. When that has been used you then refill the bottle with half water and the rest of the liquid you saved in the jar. Half-strength is half-price and it works just as well!

Saving on scouring powder
When you buy a new tin of Vim or equivalent, leave only two or three holes open at the top. This will prevent you from sprinkling out much more than you need to do the job, and the tin will last much longer. Another tip is to sprinkle the powder on to the scouring pad or cloth rather than on to the surface to be cleaned. Less powder is used in this way.

A natural air freshener
Instead of paying out for chemical air fresheners, which never seem to last very long anyway, keep fresh flowers in the rooms. If these cost too much, or you cannot grow them because you have no garden, a bouquet of common wild flowers looks most attractive and seems to bring a

breath of the countryside into your home. Many of them have the most gorgeous perfumes, too, such as meadow-sweet, woodruff, etc. Include leaves and stems to make the displays bigger. Never gather any uncommon species. Some of the commonest weeds are beautiful, such as rosebay willow-herb. Broom blossom with a few fronds of bracken looks and smells terrific.

Natural flower decorations

Although not strictly 'flowers', the most fantastic autumn and winter decorations can be made, absolutely free, from twigs, cones, dried grasses, rushes and reeds, and hedge-row berries such as hips and haws, honesty, holly, various seed pods, etc. Be sure not to gather any berries that are poisonous, such as woody and deadly nightshades, white and black bryony, etc., attractive though they may be – especially if you have children in the house, or visiting you. If you have a garden, grow everlasting flowers, gourds, and Chinese lanterns. All these can be kept indefinitely. These dried plant displays need no water, of course, so if the vase is tipped over there will be no spills to mop up.

The beautiful autumn tints of beech leaves can be preserved by standing the twigs in water to which a tablespoon or two of glycerine has been added. Leave them for two or three weeks, then remove twigs and dry the ends, and they are ready to use. The glycerine and water mixture can be used for a fresh batch. Experiment with twigs bearing the autumn-tinted leaves of other tree species.

Whitening nylon, terylene and net curtains

Don't waste money on proprietary whitening agents for these curtains. I've tried them and found that their whitening ability is negligible and they make the curtains horribly stiff, so that creases are almost impossible to iron out. Instead, put two heaped teaspoonfuls of bicarbonate of soda, and ordinary detergent powder, into hot water to wash them, rinse, and hang up to drip-dry. Do not squeeze or wring. They will come up sparkling white and need only a very light ironing.

Making disinfectant go further

Mix disinfectant with ten times the quantity of water. This makes an opaque white fluid which is quite strong enough for some jobs such as rinsing the sink and wash-basin, adding to the water when washing bedlinen and under-wear, socks, etc, to add a fresh hygienic touch, and so on. It smells hardly less strong then the undiluted original. Dettol, in particular, looks exactly like milk when diluted 1-in-10, so don't keep it in a milk bottle! *Always* label bottles containing chemicals and keep them out of reach of children and pets.

What I do is to save the empty bottles after use and put just a little of the neat product in the bottom – about half an inch – and then fill to the top with cold water. The old bottles retain their original labels, so a mistake cannot occur.

Shining lino and vinyl tiles

When washing lino and vinyl-tiled floors, dissolve a lump of sugar in the water. The floors will come up shining as though polished.

Save on stair carpeting

Allow a foot or two of spare carpeting at the top or bottom of the stairs. Then, every year when spring-cleaning, move the carpet a few inches up, or down, as the case may be, and re-fix in position. This will do much to save wear and tear on the edges of the treads where there is most wear.

Saving wear on room carpeting

On the same principle as in the previous tip, save wear and tear on a room carpet either by moving the furniture around if the room has a fitted carpet, or turning the carpet round if it is a 'loose' square. Change the positions of rugs, too, or you'll find the part surrounding the rug is faded by comparison with the part that is under the rug, when you *do* move it. The carpet pile under the rug will also be flattened.

Save your curtains from fading
Twice a year change your curtains over – putting the left-hand curtain on the right and vice versa. This will prevent uneven fading in sunlight.

Wage war on splodge!
'Splodge' is the word coined in our family many years ago to describe things which are not in their proper place (e.g. piles of old magazines left lying around) and things which haven't been used for years but taking up space unnecessarily since they are no longer used. Be ruthless! Get rid of the lot! Clutter breeds dust, and dust encourages germs. Old newspapers have a good many uses (see Chapter 10) but if you cannot use them in any of these ways tie them in bundles and send them for recycling. Some councils collect them for this purpose if you have a quantity. Magazines can be given to hospitals, ladies' hairdressers or your doctor's waiting-room. Unwanted articles can go to jumble sales, Oxfam, etc. The resulting cupboard, wall, wardrobe, shelf or floor space can be put to good use for the storage of the things you *do* need.

Cleaning grubby piano keys
If water gets between the keys the piano can be ruined. Use meths on a soft cotton rag.

Cleaning pans after cooking eggs
Don't soak the pans in hot water or you'll 'cook' the remnants of the eggs even more firmly to the bottom of the pan. Soak in *cold* water.

Removing rust from bicycle parts
Mix a little oil (any kind) with scouring powder to a sloppy paste, and brush this on the rusty frame, wheel rim or whatever. Leave it on for about twenty minutes. Then wipe off with a cloth. The rust will have disappeared.

Save Our Soles!
When you buy new shoes, fix rubber stick-on soles and heels to them before wearing. The saving on shoe repair bills, especially for children's shoes, will be enormous. When these wear out, stick on another set. This will prolong the life of the shoes almost indefinitely. Finally, when the uppers show signs of wear but are still serviceable enough to be worn, wear the original soles and heels as purchased new.

Which brings me to the cleaning angle. Preserve the leather of the uppers with dubbin, as used by hikers and mountaineers for their boots. This makes them water proof. Use a neutral shade of polish for all your shoes, thus avoiding buying several different shades.

A use for an old tea-strainer
When your tea-strainer has just about had its lot, don't throw it out. It can still do duty for a long time afterwards for lowering eggs into boiling water and fishing them out afterwards.

Drying kitchen towels
After a baking or roasting, or cooking a casserole, make use of the heat remaining in your oven by draping washed tea-towels over the oven door. They'll be dry in a jiffy.

Oven cleaning
Special oven cleaners are quite unnecessary. It's good old bicarbonate of soda again coming to the rescue! Make into a paste with water and dab it all over the surfaces to be cleaned. You don't do this after cooking (and risk burning your hands) but you put it on *before* you cook. The heat will turn the paste brown, but no matter, it's doing its job. After cooking, leave the oven to cool sufficiently, then wipe over the surfaces with a cloth wrung out in warm soapy water. All the burnt grease will literally fall off, leaving your oven sparkling clean in minutes. You don't need any harsh abrasive pads, either – just a soft cloth.

Buy only washable clothes

Don't buy clothes which can only be dry-cleaned. This costs a bomb. Many coats, suits, etc. are made in drip-dry fabrics these days and do not even need pressing after a dip in the wash-tub.

Cleaning mirrors

A few drops of meths on a soft cotton cloth will bring up a beautiful depth and sparkle in mirrors. Polish with a clean dry cloth afterwards.

Cleaning stained aluminium pans

Boil rhubarb or apple peelings in water in a stained aluminium pan and it will come up brilliantly clean.

Cleaning burnt saucepans

Soak the pan with a solution of washing detergent in hot water overnight. The next day bring to the boil, then reduce heat and let it simmer for about half an hour (sounds like a cookery recipe!) The burnt food will then be loosened and come off very easily with your washing-up brush.

De-scaling furred kettles

There's no need to spend money on proprietary products for de-scaling a kettle. Fill the kettle with water and add a tablespoonful of borax or citric acid. Bring to the boil, leave for a short time, them empty and rinse well several times. This treatment can be used both for electric kettles and for the type used on a gas cooker.

Why not prevent 'fur' building up in your kettle in the first place? Once a week add a tablespoonful of vinegar to a full kettle of water and bring to the boil. Empty and rinse well. This prevents the scale forming.

Dripping tap stains

The ugly dark stains made by dripping taps on sinks and baths can be removed by rubbing the stains with half a lemon dipped in salt, leaving it on for twenty-four hours, then washing off and repeating this procedure until the stain has gone. Then change the washer in the tap to stop it dripping.

Copper pans

The very same thing – half a lemon dipped in salt – will burnish a copper pan to a bright shine. If the pan is in very bad condition you may have to repeat several times.

Make your own soap flakes

It is cheaper to buy cheap tablet soaps and grate them to make your own soap flakes for washing, if you prefer soap to synthetic detergents. Store in a screw-top jar. Boots frequently have mild soaps in packs of four as special offers, pleasantly perfumed. These make ideal soap flakes.

Cleaning a burnt milk pan

A handful of soil from the garden (or an indoor plant pot or window-box, if you have no garden) mixed with water to make ordinary mud, will clean a milk pan which has burnt black. Leave it for an hour or so, then wash it all out with boiling water. It's a funny thing, but although mud will clean the burnt pan like magic, it won't clean your son's rugby shorts and socks.

Cleaning burnt enamel pans

These do not respond to mud, so they require different treatment. Fill the pan with cold water, add a handful of cooking salt and boil for ten minutes. This works like magic! Kitchen salt can also be used to scour pans if you happen to run out of Vim.

Save time in cleaning the oven drip-tray

Line the tray with kitchen foil. When greasy and messy-looking, just lift out the foil and put it in the dustbin. You will not then need to spend ages scouring a greasy tray. Re-line with foil for the next use.

Pan scourers for free

Save the plastic netting in which supermarkets sell oranges, carrots, etc. Screwed up into a ball, they make excellent pan scourers.

Be your own Dyno-Rod

Screw a hook firmly into the end of an expanding plastic-covered wire curtain-rod, then push the rod down the pipe as far as it will go. Nine times out of ten it will clear the bend of the obstruction. For Pete's sake, though, don't let it go, or the plumber you will have to call in will have to locate your rod as well as the obstruction, and more than likely this will push up the bill.

Beetroot stains on table linen

Don't panic! Soak a slice of bread in water and lay it on a flat surface. Lay the stain over it. Then lay another similarly-soaked slice of bread over the stain. You will find that the bread will absorb the stain completely.

Improve the output of light bulbs

Clean the accumulated dust off all light bulbs regularly with a soft cloth dampened with plain water only. You will be surprised at the greater brightness of the light! Incidentally, save electricity by using lower-wattage bulbs where possible (though not, of course, to the detriment of your eyesight).

Save on hot water

Washing-up under a running tap wastes hot water. Use a washing-up bowl.

If you have an open fire, keep a large, heavy copper kettle on the hob. You will have constant hot water available for various cleaning jobs without having to use the water heated by electricity or gas. This can made an appreciable saving on the bill.

Chapter Three

The Bathroom

We ended the last chapter talking about saving on hot water. This is as good a point as any to start with in this chapter. After all, it's the bath that uses more hot water than anything. Except, of course, when you have a cold bath! Learn to like cold baths – they're absolutely fantastic for whipping up a sluggish circulation. The glow can actually be seen as well as felt when you scrub the skin with a loofah, or even an ordinary sponge. Yes, you've guessed correctly – I am a cold bath fanatic! However, I don't go in for them in order to save hot water, although of course they do – I enjoy them and use them for health reasons. (All the year round!)

Instal a shower
A cold shower is even more invigorating than a cold bath. You get a tingle as well as a glow. After a cold shower you feel fit and ready for anything, whether it's sport, study, housework, or writing books.

A hot shower uses far less hot water than a hot bath – the only time the use of *running* hot water is justified! However, the amount of hot water you save depends on how long you are in the shower, and how much water you use in a hot bath. The leisurely bath reader, who has the hot water up to his or her neck and keeps topping it up almost as fast as the pages of the book are turned, will not save as much hot water as the person who takes a bath containing only just enough water to cover the nether regions.

A girl I used to know rigged up a most ingenious device for bath-time reading. She tied a cord from the geyser to the door-handle and pegged magazines to this with spring clothes-pegs. Be warned – you will not save on your fuel bill this way, as you will be topping up the hot water as soon as it falls a few degrees while you are immersed (ouch!) in the magazine of your choice.

Joint baths for the family
Take a bath with your spouse. Bath the children together. Wash each other's hair under the shower. One bath instead of two cuts the heating bill in half. One bath instead of three cuts it by two-thirds. If you have six children you can very nearly cut it out altogether.

Dripping taps
Until such time as you can change the washer (or call in a plumber if you can't manage the job yourself), secure a face flannel to hang over the tap. The water will then run through the cloth, avoiding those nasty stains caused by dripping taps, and also the irritating noise.

Mildewed shower curtains
When plastic shower curtains show mildew, scrub with a paste made of bicarbonate of soda and water, and rinse.

A new use for an old loofah
Don't throw out the old loofah when it is on its last legs. Cut into pieces, it will make excellent scouring pads for the kitchen, and it will not scratch non-stick pans.

How to make a soap sponge
Cut a foam sponge into two halves along its length, i.e., into two narrow oblongs. Sew along three edges to make a bag, and fill with soap scraps and ends, then sew up the remaining edge. This makes a foaming sponge for use in the bath, and saves on soap, which need never be wasted.

Shopping lists from soap
No, I'm not suggesting that you carve your shopping lists on a tablet of soap! But you will find that the vast majority of toilet soaps contain an inner wrap of white cardboard

inside the outer packing. Keep these cards, which are just
the right size for a shopping list to slip into coat pocket or
handbag. Folded once, they are better for writing notes for
the milkman, too, as their stiffness makes the note become
wedged in the top of the milk bottle and not slip down
inside the bottle.

Saving on toothpaste

When a tube is almost empty, roll it as strongly as you can
from the bottom upwards with the kitchen rolling-pin,
and you will obtain enough for at least three more
brushings before throwing the empty tube away. Another
way is to rub the handle of the toothbrush up and down
the flattened tube, with a final rub upwards to extract the
loosened remnants of paste. In cold weather the paste may
be even more difficult to get out than usual; soak the tube
in hot water first before rolling.

New uses for old toothbrushes

When toothbrushes can no longer be used for their
original purpose, they make very good brushes for getting
at awkward places when cleaning, such as behind the taps
on baths, sinks and wash-basins, between the bars of
bird-cages, and so on.

Save on shampoo

Buy shampoo in the largest family economy size. Dilute
half-and-half with water when using it to wash your hair; it
will do the job just as efficiently. If you run out of
shampoo, good quality washing-up liquid is very good,
especially for greasy hair. Even the perfume of some kinds
is quite pleasant. Finally, never buy single-use sachets for
use at home – most uneconomical. However, they are ideal
for use on holiday. They weigh hardly anything (an
important consideration especially for airline luggage) and
take up much less space than bottles. They are also much
less likely to leak than bottles.

Cheap bath salts

You need a 2 lb carton of washing soda and a few empty glass jars (with lids). Divide the soda among the jars, then sprinkle in a few drops of vegetable food colouring (or, if preferred, you can colour the crystals in a bowl before putting them into the jars). Then add a few drops of eau-de-cologne or lavender water, and put on the lids.

Cotton-wool ball economy

Buy the largest size roll of cotton-wool, roll your own cotton-wool balls and put them into transparent plastic bags. Much cheaper than the pre-packed product. You can store the balls in a glass jar if you prefer. This should have a lid, to avoid dampening the wool from bathroom steam..

Saving on tissues

Instead of buying the small-size tissues, buy the large 'mansize' ones and cut them in half.

Razor-blade economy

After shaving as many times as possible with a blade, turn it over in the razor. It can be used for the same number of times on the other edge. Thus you get twice as many shaves from one blade.

Hand and body lotion

Glycerine and rose-water mixed in equal proportions makes a very good lotion at a fraction of the cost of expensively-packaged hand and body lotions.

Dry shampoo substitutes

Cornflour, baby powder or fine oatmeal can be used instead of branded dry shampoo powders. Be careful, though, when using oatmeal not to get your hair wet. Porridge is remarkably difficult to get out of the hair, as the mother of any two-year-old will confirm.

An inexpensive face pack (for greasy skin)
Most of the branded face packs look like mud in your eye –
or at least on your face. This one doesn't. Mix the yolk of
an egg with a few drops of olive oil, and apply to the face.
Leave it on for ten minutes, then rinse off with *cold* water
(you don't want to cook the egg on your face).

Egg on your face – again (for dry skin)
This time you use the white of the egg. Beat until stiff and
apply to the face. Leave this on until the skin feels as
though it has been stretched fairly tightly. Rinse off with
cold water.

Hair conditioning rinses
For brunettes, add a tablespoonful of cider vinegar to the
last rinse water. Blondes should substitute a tablespoonful
of lemon juice. Another conditioning rinse for blonde hair
is made by pouring half a pint of boiling water on to a
teaspoonful of fresh chamomile flowers (two teaspoonsful
if dried flowers are used). Leave to cool until the required
temperature is reached, then strain and use as the last
rinse.

Skin freshener
Mix equal parts of witch-hazel and rose-water. Dab on the
face after washing. This suits all types of skin.

Empty lipstick containers
Keep your spare hair grips in an empty lipstick container.
This also makes a handy container for any tablets you may
have to take, and can be carried in pocket or handbag.
Save on lipsticks by using a lip brush to get at the last
remnants of the lipstick. Then when all used you can boil
the container to clean it out ready for its new use.

More savings with cotton-wool
Before use, cotton-wool should be warmed by laying it on
the hot pipes or putting it into the airing cupboard. The
heat will make it swell up to twice its size, so use only half

the quantity you would otherwise detach from the roll, or only half a cotton-wool ball.

A new use for an old candlewick bedspread
Make an old candlewick bedspread into a set of co-ordinated bathroom mats. Cut out of the best parts of the bedspread two each of the shapes and sizes required for a bath mat, a pedestal mat and a lavatory mat. Sew the two pieces for each mat together, right sides outwards. The best pieces of the material form the upper surface of the mat, while worn pieces can form the under-sides as these will not show in use.

Softening the bath water
Tie a muslin bag of oatmeal on to one of the taps so that it dangles in the bath water. You can perfume this with a few drops of your favourite cologne if you wish.

First aid for hair rollers
When the elastic on hair rollers becomes stretched after much use, do not throw them out but buy some rolled elastic (often called shirring or dirndl elastic) from the haberdasher, and mend the rollers with this – much cheaper than buying new rollers. Secure the rollers when setting your hair with plastic cocktail sticks, which are much cheaper than proper roller-pins.

Save on medicines
Common family remedies such as aspirin, paracetamol, petroleum jelly, etc. are very much cheaper when bought as unbranded British Pharamacopoeia (BP) products from chain chemists and supermarkets, and are just as good.

Bandages for the first-aid box
Cut old worn cotton (not nylon) sheets into strips of various widths and roll up for use as bandages. Boil the sheets first, iron out flat and cut the strips, then seal the rolled strips in plastic bags. Save old cotton gloves and cut off the fingers to cover bandaged fingers; this protects the

bandage as well as the cut from dirt. Fingers cut from old rubber gloves can be used as finger-stalls to protect from water.

An effective sunburn lotion
Half a cup of milk mixed with a teaspoonful of bicarbonate of soda makes a soothing alkaline lotion. Dab gently on the affected area with cotton-wool.

Make your own first-aid box
Save a large square or oblong biscuit-tin (round ones are unsuitable). The smaller flat oblong tins in which short-bread is packed make a good size of first-aid box to keep in the glove compartment of your car.

Paint the tins on the outside with white enamel. When this has dried thoroughly, paint on a red cross in the middle, and stencil the words FIRST AID on the lid. Fill the boxes with the necessary items and keep in an easily-accessible position, one in the bathroom and one in the kitchen, and one in the car if you have one. Considerable savings may be effected by making your own bandages, finger-stalls and the box itself, and buying BP remedies instead of branded ones, as mentioned above.

Chapter Four

The Bedroom

When you think of the bedroom, the first thing that comes to mind is the bed. And here I must make a departure from the economy line. Always buy the best bed that you can afford, and never buy a secondhand bed.

Considering that we spend approximately one third of our lives in bed, it stands to reason that the bed ought to be a good one. An uncomfortable night can cause insomnia, back and joint pain, and a legacy of bad temper the following day. It's not a question of getting out of bed on the wrong side – it's usually more a question of getting out of the wrong kind of bed to suit the sleeper.

There are many kinds of bases, springs and mattresses and you should choose one to suit you. Some prefer a hard bed, some a firm one, some a softer type. Some like their bed to be high off the floor, others prefer the much lower kind. For those who like to sit on the edge, pulling on their socks or sipping a leisurely cup of tea, a firm edge is a must. Don't be embarrassed to try out a bed in the furniture store by lying on it full-length. After all, that's what a bed is for, and the salesman knows this just as much as you do. Just sitting on the side of the bed, or even prodding it with the fingers, is completely useless for giving you the kind of information you need, which is: how that particular bed will suit you when you sleep on it.

Secondhand beds, and mattresses in particular, are an abomination. *Never* buy one. First of all, they are most unhygienic. At worst they may harbour fleas or bed-bugs. These may be hidden in the interior, coming out only when a warm body is on top. Quite apart from the bites, they are also extremely difficult to get rid of. Secondly, a used mattress has been pressed to accommodate someone else's physical contours and will as likely as not be quite unsuited to your own body shape. It will have humps and lumps in all the wrong places. So make do with your old bed until you can afford to buy a new one.

Now for the good news. You can make all the economies you like with the bedding! Sheets, blankets, duvets, bedspreads – all these can cost you as little or as much as you choose. Since we are interested in economy in this book, let us take a look at some of the ways in which we can save in the bedroom. The savings we can make will go a long way to offset the outlay we have had to make on the basic bed itself.

Sheets
The time-honoured dodge of turning sides to middle when the central part of a sheet has worn thin or in holes is, to my mind, not the best way of dealing with it. Have you ever tried to sleep on a lumpy, obtrusive join? A thick seam is almost as irritating on a top sheet – a sleeper who pulls the bedclothes up to his or her head will find the joined part tickling the face! No – make the good parts into pillow-cases instead. The worn parts can be put into the rag-bag to become soft polishing pads, rags to clean the car, kitchen swabs, etc. If they are thin but not in holes they can be cut into strips for bandages.

Sheets which are too short can be lengthened by adding pieces of a contrasting or toning material, either patterned or plain. If the additional length required is only a few inches, a band of embroidered ribbon can be inserted, in the same way that lace is inserted, by cutting off the edge and joining both the cut edges to the strip to be inserted. Alternatively, a piece of some other material can be added to the bottom where it will not show.

Sheets are often available at jumble sales, frequently in very good condition, sometimes even new or nearly-new, and are usually incredibly cheap. I once bought a pair of double cotton sheets absolutely new and unused at a jumble sale for 20p. I suppose I was just lucky, as I would not expect to find a bargain like that very often! However, the majority of jumble sales usually have a selection of used sheets in good condition, which need only boiling and ironing. Odd ones can be cut in half to make cot sheets, or made into pillow-cases.

Make your own sheets. You can buy sheeting by the yard. This is much cheaper than buying ready-made sheets. All you have to do is to hem the tops and bottoms. The top hem should be wider than the one at the bottom, and can either be left plain, or bound or embroidered. Be sure that you measure the bed and buy the correct amount of material; check the width of the material as well as the length you need to purchase. Don't forget to allow for the hems, and a generous length to turn under the mattress. For the same reason the width of the material should be chosen to allow enough to turn under the mattress on each side plus the actual width of the bed. Sheeting is sold in various widths to suit single, small double (4ft) and standard double (4ft 6in) beds.

If you wish to make matching pillow-cases you must allow more material, including a few inches for the turn-in part that folds over the pillow to keep it in place inside the pillow-case. Side seams will not need a lot of material as they are usually narrow. The fold-in 'housewife' style is the easiest to make.

Blankets

The same applies to blankets as to sheets, except that you can't make pillow-cases out of the good parts of worn ones! There's not much you can do when blankets 'go' in the middle. No one would want to use a blanket with a thick join – it would be difficult to sew anyway owing to the thickness of the material. They can be cut down for cot blankets. Turn the cut edges to form a hem and oversew with blanket-stitch. Odd worn pieces are not much good as cleaning rags but they can be cut into strips and used to stuff cushions and soft toys.

If you want to lengthen a too-short blanket by adding a piece at the bottom, be sure that the new material you use is the same thickness and weight as the blanket.

Blankets are often available cheaply at jumble sales. Look them over very carefully. That large stain where some careless person knocked over a cup of coffee several years ago will not come out, because to get a stain out you have to deal with it immediately. If you leave it for several months, never mind years, it will just become further and further ingrained into the material and impossible to remove. The secondhand blanket bargain must also be thoroughly cleaned. A dowsing in a washing-machine full of suds will often fluff up an old blanket to an incredible degree, and it is cheaper than sending it to the dry cleaners. A little bleach in the machine will whiten a dingy blanket, but do not overdo it. Strong bleaches can rot fabrics, especially if the material has had a lot of wear already.

Blanket material can be bought and can be made up to fit the bed size required. The edges can be bound with satin ribbon, or hem-stitched with blanket-stitch. Either way this will be much cheaper than buying ready-made blankets.

Bedspreads

Somehow jumble sale bedspreads always seem to look tatty. A much nicer idea is to make a patchwork bedspread. This need not cost you anything if you have lots of spare pieces of material in your rag-bag, provided that they are all of more or less the same weight and thickness. The easiest and quickest way to make a patchwork bedspread is to cut the fabric into squares and join them on the sewing-machine. You can arrange them in regular alternating patterns, or join them random fashion – the choice is yours. A minimum size of 6-inch squares will help reduce the amount of work by avoiding too many small squares – if your fabric pieces are big enough, 8-inch squares are even better as this will reduce the number of squares to be joined even further.

If you are a keen knitter or crocheter, you can knit or crochet the squares from oddments of wool, and join them to make a heavier winter bedspread.

Another idea, especially if you like crafts and sewing, is to make the basic spread from plain material and decorate it with appliqué patches cut in floral or other shapes. A child's bedspread could be decorated with appliqué animals, footballs, teddy bears or other figures. Draw the figure on a piece of paper in the size required and cut round it to form a pattern, then pin this to your material and cut it out, allowing a quarter-inch for turning the raw edge under. Oversew with blanket-stitch.

Duvet covers

I do not recommend you try to make your own duvet, as this is a difficult undertaking. It is better to buy the basic duvet, and make your own covers.

Machine patchwork is ideal for duvet covers. Measure the size required, and cut a piece of plain material for one side. This will be the underside which does not normally show when on the bed (you thus avoid the work of doing twice as much square-sewing as you need to do if you have both sides of the cover made of patchwork). Cut out 8-inch (or 6-inch) squares of your fabric for the patchwork, make the upper side of the duvet cover, then stitch all round on the reverse side, leaving an opening at the top big enough to get the duvet into. Measure this opening and attach a lightweight zip fastener, choosing one of the colours of the patchwork pieces. Press the seams of the patchwork out on the reverse side *before* stitching the patchwork side of the duvet cover to the plain side. Then press both on the outside.

Babies' cot quilt covers can be made in the same way. As they are so much smaller, you can use 4-inch squares, as very large squares look out of proportion on a tiny quilt. Why not make the complete quilt? It is very easy when using the polyester foam wadding which is sold by the yard for the purpose of making fillings for quilts, quilted clothes, stuffed toys etc. It is very cheap – I paid 29p a yard for it when I was making some quilts for babies' prams and cots. All you have to do is to cut this material to the exact size of the two halves of your quilt cover, and lay it on the inside, on top of the two pieces you have ready to join together on the machine. Pin them all together half an inch from the edge, and machine them a quarter-inch from the edge, outside the line of the pins. The foam is very easy to machine through, and does not fray.

When all three pieces have been thus joined, pull out the pins and cut round the edge so that no foam sticks out beyond the edge of the material, which it sometimes does when flattened by the seaming. Then turn the right way out and press. The quilt is ready when you have sewn up the side you left open for turning. It is easiest if you leave open the top edge (one of the short edges), cut away any excess foam and turn in the edge of the plain side, pinning it in place, and hem with tiny stitches, using invisible nylon thread.

When I made these quilts I made matching pillow-cases from one of the materials used, to tone with the colour scheme.

This foam is completely washable both by hand and in the washing-machine.

Recycle your nightdresses
When your nightdress has worn out, cut off the worn top part, thread elastic through a hem made at the waist, and you have a waist slip. You can adjust the length from the top, then you do not need to cut the bottom edge. Add a lace edging if you wish.

An old nightdress can also be unpicked and made into children's undergarments.

Recycle your old pyjamas
A worn pair of pyjamas can be cut down to make a child's pyjamas. It is easier to unpick the whole thing and use a proper paper pattern than to try to juggle with cutting necklines, sleeves, armholes and so on smaller.

Uses for old containers
Make fancy containers for combs, slides, hair grips, costume jewellery, etc. by saving the coloured plastic tops

from used hair lacquer sprays. You can also re-use empty washing-up liquid containers by cutting them in half and enamelling the bottom half. Tissue containers can be covered with fancy paper or material and re-used for tissues. You then buy the supermarket own-brand tissues which are put up in cellophane bags at half the price of boxed tissues, to refill the decorated tissue container. Adhesive plastic such as Fablon can also be used, and is stronger than ordinary paper or fabric.

Cheaper night lights
Cut an ordinary candle into six pieces. Each makes one night light, and is much cheaper than buying six of these items put up in packets. Pare the wax in the centre of the five lower pieces to expose the wick. A sharp-pointed knife will do this job very easily. Stand each night light on a saucer when required for use.

Space-saving in the wardrobe
Attach plastic suction hooks to the inside of the rear wall of the wardrobe and inside the doors, and you can then hang up items such as shoes, stockings and tights, scarves, gloves, etc. in plastic carrier bags to save space on shelves and in drawers. Label the bags for quick identification.

A linen chest for bedroom storage
Buy a old wooden chest at a jumble sale or in a junk shop. An old baggage trunk would do. Cover with cloth to match your curtains. Make a large foam cushion the same size as the lid, and you will have a useful article – a seat in the bedroom which also contains your spare blankets, sheets, etc.

Saving at the linen sales
Unbleached twill sheets, or sheeting, looks rather drab when first bought, but soon washes white. It's considerably cheaper than white sheets and sheeting. After a few boilings it comes up very nicely.

Bedside rugs for free
Ask carpet shops for their out-of-date, unwanted carpet sample books and swatches. These contain sample pieces of discontinued lines. They are usually only to glad to get rid of them, since if they are no longer in use they are just taking up space. Why not let them take up space on your bedroom floor?

The samples are normally in good-sized squares or oblongs. Choose enough of them, in toning or contrasting colours, to make a patchwork rug of the size required, and join the pieces together with carpet tape and Copydex.

Some enterprising thrift freaks have carpeted whole rooms with these sample pieces in eye-catching check designs, but they must have had lots of time to go round all the carpet firms and also been lucky enough to find several firms who had the books to give away all at the same time! One could, of course, stockpile them a few at a time, but that might pose a storage problem.

Making your own rugs
The cost of making a rug using a rug kit is more than that of buying a ready-made rug, so this is for the birds, unless you happen to be a rugmaking craft enthusiast. However, you can make a rug much more economically by buying just the rug canvas and a hook, and cutting old stockings and tights into strips. These are then looped through the canvas just like rug wool. The various shades of the nylons will produce a pleasant variegated effect, but if you particularly want the rug to be all in one shade, just boil all the nylons together in a large pot of plain water. No dye is needed. When boiled for about half an hour, they will be all the same shade.

A rug made with nylon loops in this way will be very springy, and also hard-wearing.

You can also knit or crochet rugs, using very thick wool. Patterns for eye-catching designs are frequently given in women's magazines. If you don't want to bother with a pattern, just knit squares and join them (or crochet them), and sew the finished rug on to a backing of hessian for stability.

Save on carpet underlay

A bedroom carpet usually has less wear and tear than a living-room carpet and, while it is not a real economy to skimp on the underlay for a living-room carpet, it is not really necessary to spend money on an underlay for the bedroom carpet. Just cover the floor with several layers of newspaper. This has the additional advantage of being good insulating material, and therefore promoting warmth.

Curtains from sheets

Sheets can be made into curtains, if you have enough material. Just dye the material whatever shade you need to go with your bedroom décor, and cut to size. Hem the bottoms and add rufflette tapes to the top edges.

Hot-water bottle lore

When using a new hot-water bottle for the first time, add a few drops of glycerine the first time you fill it. This will make the bottle last much longer.

When the bottle leaks, don't consign it to the dustbin. Cut off the top, stuff with old tights and re-seal the top with tape and rubber solution. You have now made a very good kneeling-mat for scrubbing and polishing the floor, or weeding the garden.

A tie rack in the wardrobe

A length of white plastic-covered spring wire curtain rod stretched between two small hooks on the inside of the wardrobe door makes an ideal tie rack.

A new idea for worn pillow-cases

If a pillow-case has become worn in the middle, put a piece of contrasting material into a diamond-shape and stitch it over the centre of the pillow-case. This will not only decorate but also strengthen the pillow-case.

Lengthening shrunken curtains
If your bedroom curtains have shrunk in the wash, they
can be lengthened most attractively by sewing lampshade
fringing along the bottom.

Bedside mats from rugs
Do not throw out your rugs when they become worn thin
in the middle. Cut off the two good ends, which will make
a pair of bedside mats, or two slip mats to put inside the
door.

A bedroom water bottle
An old wine carafe with a glass reversed over the top
makes a very attractive bedside table water bottle. Choose
a straight-sided glass, if possible one with a rounded base.
These are rather difficult to find now but sometimes turn
up in jumble sales.

Chapter Five

The Nursery

The cost of providing all the items needed by a baby – especially a first baby – can be drastically cut by recycling existing items. The results are perfectly acceptable even to the most caring and conscientious parents. The only hurdle to be overcome is the very understandable one of parents insisting that everything for the new baby must be new, too. First-time parents are particularly prone to this budget-wrecking syndrome.

Since the most dramatic savings will be made by finding alternative substitutes for the biggest items such as cots, prams, baths, etc., we will start with those. More than half the items which excited first-time parents rush out to buy – at exorbitant prices – can be recycled from existing materials or adapted from other items. A good many of the things for which parents frequently incur a great financial burden are frankly unnecessary.

The cot
To buy a small-size crib, treasure cot or Moses basket for the new baby and then a full-size drop-side cot afterwards is sheer madness. The new baby will grow too big for the snug little nest almost before you can say goo-goo-goo. In just a matter of weeks his or her head will touch one end and feet the other. Babies grow amazingly quickly, especially in the first few months.

The most practical idea is to buy secondhand a full-size drop-side cot, which will last you (or rather, the baby) until he or she is ready for a proper bed, somewhere around the age of two. Do not, however, be tempted to economize to the extent of doing without the cot. A drop-side barred cot is the safest place for a toddler, especially if

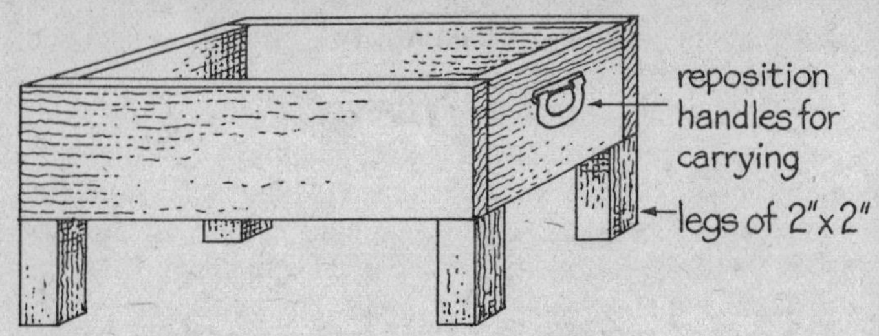

Fig. 1

he or she decides to toddle in the middle of the night or at some other time when you are not looking.

If you absolutely insist on putting baby into something smaller to start with, a large drawer from a full-size chest of drawers can be adapted to form a cosy crib for the first few weeks. Such a drawer is normally bigger in any case than the usual size of the cribs available for sale, and will therefore last the baby longer as well as having more room both widthways and lengthways.

Take the two handles off the front of the drawer and reposition them at the ends (i.e. on the short sides). You have now made the drawer into a carry-cot!

The best place to stand it is on a low table, but should you not have a suitable table available you can adapt it for standing on the floor by adding legs of two-by-two (Fig.1). These should be *very firmly* screwed to the four corners from the inside of the drawer bottom. The legs need not be very tall, but high enough to keep the drawer well above floor level; if stood directly on the floor the crib would be susceptible to draughts. A mat or rug should be laid on the floor first under the crib.

When baby has graduated to a full-size cot, your crib can become a drawer again by unscrewing the legs and re-siting the handles in their original positions. The holes in the bottom made by the screws can be filled with plastic wood, and the marks left when removing the handles from the two ends can be filled in likewise. In any case these will not show when the drawer is in normal use.

I once knew a family who had to take *three* drawers out of their tallboy – they had triplets!

As I mentioned earlier, the full-size drop-side cot can be purchased secondhand. Private small-ads in the local newspaper seem to be the best source if you want to find one in good condition. A good many of the ones I have seen in secondhand shops looked rather grotty. If sanded and painted to an attractive shade, your bargain will be just as good as a new one and cost far less. You can add nursery transfers if you wish, unless the cot is the type with bars all the way round with no solid part in the middle at the ends.

Bedding

You can make a mattress to fit the drawer-crib by recycling a full-size (adult) pillow-case. Stuff the pillow-case with a slab of foam rubber, which is washable and hygienic. The slab should be cut 1/8th inch smaller all round than the pillow-case. It should then be *sewn* into the pillow-case to avoid its becoming dislodged if the baby wriggles about, or during washing. A slightly larger pillow-case can then be slipped over this as a loose, washable mattress-cover.

Between the two you can slip the usual waterproof sheet. Use only a proper plastic or rubber sheet sold for the purpose, and do not be tempted to economize by using a heavy plastic bag. It cannot be emphasized too often that plastic bags of any kind must *never* be used for any purpose connected with babies and children. To be on the safe side, sew four tapes to the corners of the waterproof sheet and tie them together on the underside of the mattress before slipping on the mattress cover. The cover itself should also fasten in some way, e.g. with press studs, so that it cannot slip off in use.

A mattress for a full-size drop-side cot can be made from a larger and thicker slab of foam rubber. Make a bag from old sheeting which will be just 1/8th inch bigger than the slab all round when the edges have been seamed together, insert the slab and sew it in as before. Then make a loose mattress cover, also from an old sheet, in the same style as that for the drawer-crib, i.e., like a slip-in pillow-case, fastened by press studs.

Sets of sheets for the drawer-crib and the drop-side cot can be made from an ordinary bedsheet which has worn thin in the middle. Instead of turning sides to middle and enduring the discomfort of the hard join, which always seem to be able to bore through even the thickest pyjamas, it will do much better duty as two pairs of cot sheets or three pairs of crib sheets. Cut the sheet into four equal pieces, if single (six pieces if double) and hem the sides, tops and bottoms either by hand or machine, after first cutting off the worn portions.

A young baby does not need a pillow, so that is an item you do not have to worry about until the child graduates to a full-size cot; even then the pillow should be as flat as possible. Make the pillow in the same way from old sheeting, using the thinnest possible slab of foam rubber as a filling. Make sure that the foam rubber is sewn strongly into the covering bag. Pillow-cases are, of course, made from old sheets. If you are short of old sheets, a good source of supply is jumble sales, where I have seeen full-size double sheets in good condition go for as little as 10p. All you have to do is to boil them, iron them and start cutting! Don't use nylon sheets, which are unhealthily overheating and non-absorbent; use only cotton, linen or terylene. The latter are very good, because they are drip-dry and minimum-iron, and are smooth and soft to use.

Blankets can be cut out of old worn ones. These can similarly be found at jumble sales, if you haven't any old ones you no longer use. There is usually an assortment of sizes and colours, and rarely does any one item cost more than about 25p. They should always be washed or dry cleaned before use – not only as a hygienic precaution but also because they frequently come up like new afterwards. After cutting to size, they can be blanket-stitched round the edges, or they may be bound with ribbon, as you prefer.

Cot covers are a matter of personal taste. You can use a colourful plaid blanket, or you can make a patchwork quilt from scraps. It is quite simple to make one of these from squares of material – you do not need templates or elaborate shapes for the patches. Twenty-four squares each 4½ inches will make the top surface. Join on the machine with ¼ inch turnings all round. Then add a plain backing sheet using a piece of material to pick up the colour or design (or both) of one of the patches used in your design. An easy design is made by using squares in three different materials in a repetitive sequence. The first row will be: 1, 2, 3, 1, 2, 3. The second row will be: 3, 1, 2, 3, 1, 2. The third row will be: 2, 3, 1, 2, 3, 1, and the fourth row will be: 1, 2, 3, 1, 2, 3. This will give you a diagonal design running through the squares (see Fig. 2 which shows this clearly).

When you have joined top and reverse side around three edges to make a bag, cut a piece of terylene wadding the

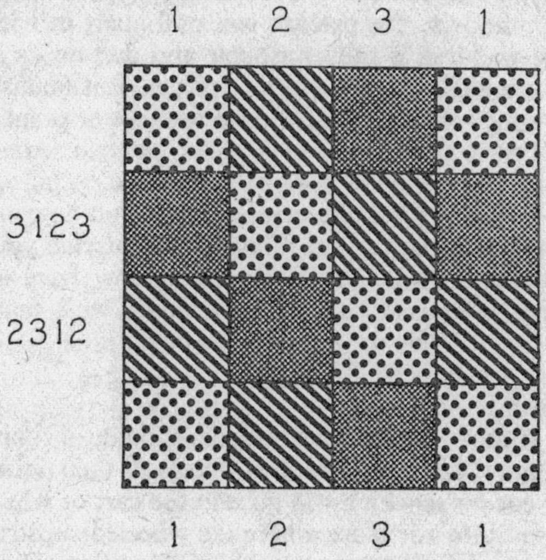

Fig. 2   Simple patchwork using 3 materials

exact size of your quilt cover (which will be approximately 24 inches by 16 inches). Machine this all round three sides (not at the open end) making sure that the machine does not run off the edge – the wadding must be *firmly* attached to the quilt cover or it will come adrift and buckle up when the quilt is washed. If you are an experienced needle-woman you can pin all three layers together (the quilt cover pieces facing, the wadding layer on top) and machine all three together at one go. Then turn the quilt cover the right way out, which will leave the filling layer in the middle. The open end will then have to be stitched neatly by hand. To do this as unobtrusively as possible, fold the edge of the top (the squared side) over narrowly once and then again, and pin in position over the folded edge of the reverse side. Stitch neatly with so-called 'invisible' (colourless) nylon thread.

The only important rule is to use materials of the same thickness and texture for your patches. Use all cottons, all poplins, all synthetics, etc. but not a heterogeneous hodge-podge, otherwise the patches will pull apart in use. The terylene wadding is fully washable and despite its fragile appearance will not fray or fall to pieces. It is fantastically cheap – one yard at 29p will make four cot or pram quilts and still leave some pieces over which can be used to stuff a cot pillow, soft toy or for some other use. A pillow-case can be made to match the reverse side if you have enough material, otherwise use one of the other materials you have used in making the patchwork. You now have a very attractive reversible and washable quilt with matching pillow-case suitable for the crib, cot or pram.

The pram
It goes without saying that the pram should, of course, be one of those 'carry-cot' types on wheels. It then doubles as a carry-cot *per se* which will go into the car, or which can be carried into any place where the wheeled substructure makes it impracticable to take the whole thing. The same mattress and bedding will do for both drawer-crib and pram, and when the child is too big for the drawer-crib the

crib mattress then does duty as a pram mattress, along with the crib bedding to start with and the cot bedding when the baby is bigger.

The bath

The purpose-made baby bath on a stand may be very convenient but it will not last more than a few weeks as the baby will very soon outgrow it. An oval washing-up bowl is probably the most convenient thing to use to start with. Large plastic ones are still quite cheap and after baby has outgrown it you can of course use it for washing-up, etc. in the kitchen. Stand the bowl on a low table, and lay a terry towel or nappy on the bottom before pouring the water in. This is to stop baby from sliding about and slipping.

When baby is too big for the plastic bowl, the kitchen sink makes a good intermediate stage before graduating to the adult bath. Turn off the taps very tightly and push the plug in very firmly so that inquisitive fingers will not meddle with them. The plug must be covered with a pad to avoid any metal parts coming in contact with the baby. The metal taps must also be well-padded for protection. Foam rubber is as good as anything and pieces of this material can be tied on with tapes. Don't forget the non-slip mat – a towel or nappy.

The potty

I cannot think of a single object for this purpose which does not have sharp edges, so you will have to buy this item. The modern nursery potty is purpose-built for the job, shaped to fit a baby's bottom and made to stand firmly on the floor without overturning. Being plastic, they are also hygienic as they can be rinsed with boiling water and Dettol.

Nappies

From the potty to nappies is but a short step. *Good quality* disposable nappy liners can be used again and again provided that they are only wet, not soiled, and are thoroughly rinsed and sterilized after each use. Buying good quality disposables is really an economy, because the cheap ones will not stand up to re-use; in some cases they are so flimsy that they barely stand up to one use!

The sterilizing solution that you use for your baby's feeding bottles can be used only once, and after the bottle has been treated the used sterilizing solution should be used for soaking nappies. Dilute it with more water and put the nappies into the solution in a lidded plastic bucket. By the time you are ready to wash them properly they will be sterile and halfway clean. The solution also has a whitening effect. As you know, harsh bleaches and detergents should never be used for babies' nappies as the chemicals in them can cause nappy rash and other skin problems.

Terry towelling nappies are economical in that they are constantly re-used and not destroyed, but it is best to use disposable liners inside them. This really does save you a lot of work, as soiled liners are simply destroyed (some kinds can be flushed down the toilet) and the terry ones soaked and washed in the manner described above. When baby is out of nappies, the terry ones can be put away into storage ready for the next baby or, if there isn't another addition to your family, they can be recycled into kitchen towels, face cloths, toddlers' underpants or pilch knickers, etc. You may not need twenty-four face cloths or twenty-four pairs of children's knickers – in which case join them all end to end and you will have a nice absorbent roller towel for the kitchen!

The layette
Many parents rush out and buy vast quantities of clothes for the expected new baby, completely overlooking the fact that in the vast majority of cases fond aunts and doting grandmothers will knit, crochet and embroider huge piles of bonnets, mittens, socks, matinee jackets, leggings, pram sets, and even fluffy shawls if they have the patience to cast on four or five hundred stitches and the staying-power to knit their plodding way through the uncountable rows. The worst thing about this mass of good intentions

is that half the garments will be too small in a month or two! When your relations and friends tell you they are going to knit clothes for the new baby, persuade them to make second or even third-size garments. That way you will have first-size garments from those who surprise you by not telling you beforehand, and garments in the larger sizes ready for when baby grows bigger from those who do.

The basic essentials – apart from terry nappies and disposables – are vests, nightgowns and day gowns (cotton in summer and flannel or flannelette in winter). Flannel petticoats to wear under the gowns are useful, especially in cold weather, but some mothers do not bother with them, saying that they only create more washing. If a baby is well wrapped in a shawl, mittens and socks are not really necessary. A bonnet need not be worn in summer. Matinee jackets and leggings are not really needed until the baby is several months old and can sit up unaided in the pram. If no one donates a shawl, don't panic – you do not need to knit one! A warm blanket is perfectly adequate.

When buying baby clothes, try the chain stores, which usually have good quality garments at reasonable prices. Terry nappies can be purchased at white sales, which frequently offer 'seconds' of better-quality brands. These are a real economy. After all, if one or two of them have irregular lines of stitching at the edges, baby isn't going to sue you. And if you buy cheap quality nappies they will wear so thin that when the time comes for you to recycle them they will be fit only for floor cloths and kitchen swabs.

Nursery furnishings
The beautiful dimity and spotted muslin drapes which you admire so much in the high-street showrooms are horrendously unhygienic. Those treasure cot curtains and frills and flounces attract dust and soon look very off-white indeed. They also offer a haven for flies, spiders, midges, wasps, daddy-longlegs and anything else that happens to be around in summer looking for a nice fold of material in

which to hide to escape the heat. Plain and simple should be your watchword.

The same applies to the decorations of the nursery itself. Delicate pastel wallpapers soon begin to look scruffy, and the ones with patterns of elves and bunnies are too 'twee' and babyish for a child once he or she is past the baby stage. A more practical choice would be a light, attractive floral design on a darker background that does not show up every jammy smudge and sticky finger-mark. Anyway, why use wallpaper at all? Why not paint the walls with washable satin-finish emulsion instead? You can always paper the room when baby has become a strapping teenager. Choose warm, attractive shades, which should be soothing to the eye – no garish primary colours.

As far as curtains are concerned, choose good strong, sturdy materials, not flimsy stuff. Babies are scarcely out of their cots when they start tugging at the curtains – these are usually the first objects they make a bee-line for when they begin to crawl and explore the room. The curtains should therefore be made to fall only to the window-ledge – *not* floor-length.

You can recycle any attractive substantial material into curtains for the nursery. Old linen sheets dyed make splendid nursery curtains. But, whatever you do, ensure that the hooks and rings cannot fall off. There is nothing worse than when , having washed and ironed the curtains, you are putting them up again only to find that two of the hooks have disappeared, and for ever afterwards you wonder whether one of the children is walking around containing the missing hooks. Nothing short of using a metal detector will set your mind at rest . . .

Woodwork such as doors, skirtings and window-ledges should be painted in a toning shade of lead-free gloss paint. A quick wipe-down with a damp rag will dispose of any dirty marks at one fell swoop. *Never* leave a key in the door – many toddlers have an infuriating habit of locking themselves in just to annoy!

When drawing with wax crayons becomes the rage in the nursery, you can (hopefully) avoid the walls, whether painted or papered, becoming the budding artist's canvas, by putting up a bulletin board on which paper for drawing and painting can be attached with drawing-pins. A bulletin board can be made from spare cork tiles left over after a floor-tiling job. Just glue them direct to the wall, edge-to-edge, to cover as large a space as required. This of course becomes a permanent feature, but your teenager will thank you for it when needing a bulletin board for school sports fixtures, homework schedules and youth club notices. Don't make a bulletin board from polystyrene ceiling tiles – they crumble at the edges and look most unsightly.

A blackboard may be preferred, perhaps; this item is easily made from an ordinary piece of wood or blockboard of the required size painted with matt black paint sold specially for the purpose. A narrow ledge should be screwed to the bottom to hold chalks and catch chalk dust, and a sponge should be provided for rubbing out. A damp sponge is much better than the traditional school-type blackboard rubber, which showers the user with chalk dust. Attach a tin can to one end of the ledge at the bottom of the blackboard, painted inside and out to prevent rust, as a holder for the moist sponge.

Not every parent may know that newspaper printing works sell off rolls of surplus unprinted newsprint paper at rock bottom prices. I have even known of a few that gave away ends of rolls free. This is very good paper for little children to use for their first artistic efforts.

A nursery floor is not the best place for wall-to-wall carpeting. A bare floor can be sanded, stained and sealed, and provided with tumbletwist throw rugs (which are easily washed) in strategic places. If you prefer, you can cover the floor with self-lay vinyl tiles, or tile-patterned vinyl floor covering. These materials are very easy to cut to size and lay, and certainly involve far less moil and toil – not to mention dust – than sanding, staining and sealing. Avoid a carpet in the nursery. Not only will it be trampled into oblivion, but it will receive far more than its fair share of ground-in biscuit bits, chewing-gum, plasticine, overturned paint-pot water, food and drink thrown around when baby is in one of his frustrated rages, and pee when baby is caught short. You don't really want to spend your baby's formative years on your hands and knees with a dustpan and brush instead of playing with him.

Nearly all furniture for the nursery can be recycled from second-hand items, scrubbed and repainted, or stained and polished if you prefer. Chests of drawers are more useful in the early years than wardrobes, but if you spot a bargain wardrobe nab it before someone else beats you to it. Baby will grow into clothes that need hanging up soon enough. Make sure that drawer handles and wardrobe catches are attached firmly, and that there are no keys or other loose parts which can be swallowed. Chairs should not be too high for toddlers to use. A low table is always appreciated for playing with games, puzzles and toys such as building blocks and Lego. An ordinary kitchen table can be made into a nursery table by sawing off the legs so that the top of the table is at child-height. Owing to their construction, chairs cannot really be made lower in this way, and you will need to look for low-slung children's chairs. I've always found, though, that nearly all children seem to prefer playing on the floor, whether as toddlers with their early toys and books, or later on with their train sets and racing-car tracks. And, of course, a table isn't really the ideal place for staging mock battles with Action Man, or the sets of soldiers that Dad had as a boy and has just unearthed from the attic. After all, if the defenders were to retreat too far they'd end up falling off the edge.

Chapter Six

The Playgroup

Playgroup leaders are often hard put to it to think of ways of keeping toddlers constructively occupied without the need for purchasing expensive educational toys. This chapter gives you lots of ideas for ways of keeping children of this age-group busy at literally rock-bottom cost – in some cases at no cost at all. This is an important factor to take into account for those who are trying to start a new playgroup, or to keep an existing group going, in the face of financial limitations.

It is a fallacy to imagine that small children must have elaborate or costly toys to maintain their interest. Not so. I once saw a three-year-old boy, given a very attractive constructional toy for his birthday, unwrap it as he sat on the floor, put it down on the mat and then spend the next hour playing with the box in which it had been packed. Meanwhile, his older sister took a great fancy to the decorative wrapping paper, grabbed her little pair of blunt-ended scissors and within minutes was completely absorbed in cutting out the tiny figures of Mickey Mouse, Tom and Jerry, Bugs Bunny, Tweetie Pie and other Disney characters with which the paper was printed.

Since paper and boxes are so fascinating to the two-to-fives, here are some ideas.

Ideas for very large boxes
Really huge cardboard boxes such as can easily be obtained free from wholesalers, cash-and-carry depots and bulk-buy firms make splendid houses, shops, garages, railway stations, signal-boxes, fire-stations, hospitals, schools – in fact anything a child's vivid imagination can think of. I have even known them to be used as space-ships, warships and submarines by older children!

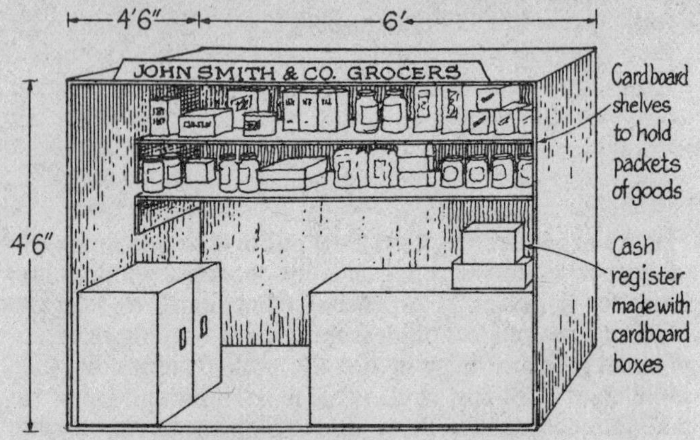

Fridge and counter made from cardboard boxes,
shop made from large carton that contained fridge or freezer

Fig. 3

Wooden boxes should never be used; they are usually bristling with protruding nails and screws and sharp edges – tea chests are the worst. A child dashing madly about in excitement can easily give himself or herself a nasty knock on the edge or corner of a wooden box. There are plenty of other things wooden boxes can be made into!

More large boxes and a few smaller ones from the supermarket will be needed to make fittings. Children love things to be realistic. An empty 'shop' will not be half so much fun as one containing counters, shelves, a fridge and a cash register, all of which can be made from cardboard boxes of appropriate size. Fig. 3 shows how to construct a counter, upon which can be ranged empty tins and packets saved from the kitchen. Do not fill them with sweets or you'll ruin the children's teeth and appetites! The counter should be made from good substantial cardboard – flimsy stuff will not support the weight of the 'goods' without sagging in the middle. Packets can be sealed with Sellotape; if they are so light they are are easily knocked over, they can be stuffed with newspaper. Do *not* weight them with pebbles or other objects which can get into toddlers' mouths. Tins should be carefully re-sealed with tape and the cut edges very strongly bound several times. If the edge is too jagged, throw it away.

Shelves are made simply by fixing lengths of strong cardboard to the inner walls with sellotape. A fridge can be made by finding a box of suitable size, making a drop-type lid from a piece of cardboard and hinging it along one side with strong tape, and then painting the whole thing white. A cash register can be made quite easily from two boxes by following the diagram at Fig. 4.

In this age-group, I would advise against allowing the children to 'sell' bottled goods in their 'shop'. Glass is so easily broken. The children will be quite happy with tins and boxes or packets which once contained jellies, beans, cocoa, tea, coffee, biscuits, etc. and you will not have anything to worry about.

The outside of the large box which the children play in can of course be painted, or covered with paper, but many children of this age-group will not bother very much what the outside looks like so long as they can get into it! Doors are easily made by cutting out an oblong panel and hinging it on down one side with strong tape. Don't attempt to

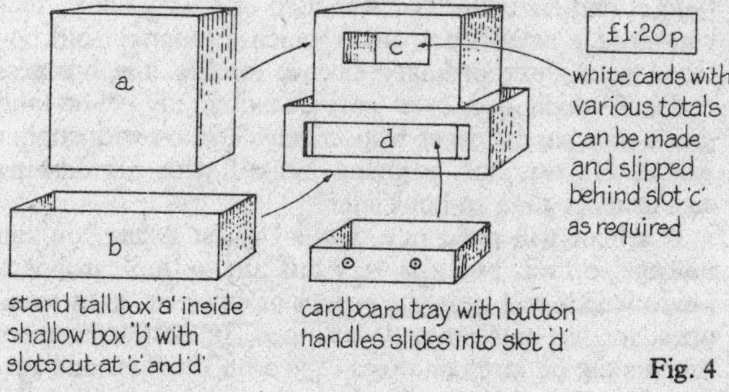

stand tall box 'a' inside shallow box 'b' with slots cut at 'c' and 'd'

cardboard tray with button handles slides into slot 'd'

Fig. 4

attach any fastening device. Windows can be cut out and either left open or filled in with sheet celluloid or acetate. *Never use plastic bags or other flexible plastic sheet for this purpose.* I cannot emphasize this too strongly. For food bags and carrier bags for the children to use for the 'goods', paper bags only should be used. A good carrier bag can be made by fastening two lengths of cotton tape to the top edges of a large strong paper bag. *Never in any circumstances give children plastic bags to play with.*

If the large box is to be used as a garage, cars can be contrived from large flattish cardboard boxes in which the toddlers can shuffle along the floor or push one another around. Features such as wheels can be painted on the outside with a felt-tip marker pen. A petrol pump can be made from a very tall narrow box. A piece of paper marked with gallon measures can be pasted on the outside, and the legs of ladies' discarded tights and stockings can be joined together into long tubes and stuffed with rolled-up newspapers to form petrol pipes! The top end is simply Sellotaped strongly to the top of the pump.

I once saw a bus made from a huge box with windows and doors cut out, with no fewer than six three-year-olds inside, including the driver! 'Where's the conductor?' I asked. 'Oh, he's gone for his tea-break!' was the reply. There's ingenuity for you.

The same bus had done duty as a railway station the day before, and a smaller box was used as a signal-box. This contained a small stool, upon which a four-year-old boy stood with three ordinary electric torches, the business ends of which had been covered with red, yellow and green transparent paper respectively, held on with rubber bands. He was still enjoying himself with his flashing signals more than an hour later!

A school will need one of the biggest boxes you can manage to find, but it is very difficult to find cardboard boxes which will bear the weight of children, even small ones, for use as seats and desk-tops. In African country schools the children sit cross-legged on the floor and rest their books on their knees; perhaps this method will be the easiest to use! You can also get far more children into the 'classroom' in this way than if you fill it with 'furniture'! Most playgroups have a small toy blackboard and easel which can be used to impart an authentic atmosphere.

You will also need a very large box to become a hospital. In fact, both for this and for a school, two large boxes joined together with Sellotape may be required, especially if there are several children. A good strong coffee-table can be used as an 'operating table', covered with an old white sheet or tablecloth. Many toddlers will prefer to use their dolls and teddy bears as 'patients', on the principle that the more the merrier, whereas if they used only themselves they could probably get only one or two children into hospital as patients, especially with the need for at least some of the children to be 'doctors' and 'nurses'! Flattish boxes will make good 'cots', and beds can be made up in them with old sheets, blankets and cushions. Smaller boxes make 'lockers'.

A wag has just told me that if there are too many children to get into the box, some can stand outside as COHSE pickets!

Smaller cardboard boxes
We now come to boxes which are too small for children to play *in* but just right for them to play *with*. A make-believe cinema, theatre or TV set can be made quite easily from ordinary cardboard supermarket boxes. The actors on the stage of the theatre will be puppets (which we will come to later) and the 'films' shown on the cinema or TV screen will be long strips of paper, with the pictures either drawn or cut out and pasted on, operated by a roller at each end. The rollers themselves are simply cut from old broomstick handles, if the 'screen' is a large one, but for a small one the cardboard rolls from the insides of kitchen paper towel rolls are ideal. The 'film' is glued to the roller at each end, and then rolled up ready for showing. The roller is merely twiddled with the fingers for this purpose – there are no spools or other complications. The rollers should, however, be firmly fixed to stand vertically at each side of a

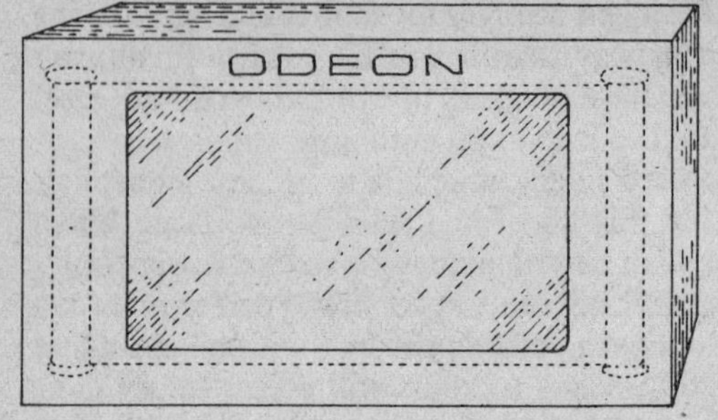

Fig. 5

'cinema screen', or centrally at the back of a 'TV screen'. For diagrams showing how to cut out boxes and fix the rollers to make the toy cinema and TV set, see Figs. 5 and 6.

The theatre does not need rollers for 'film projection' but to be realistic there should be a 'curtain' to go up and come down before and after the 'performance'. In this case the roller, which can be made of the same materials as those described above for the cinema and TV set, is attached horizontally at the top above the 'stage', and the 'curtain', which can be made of paper or cloth, is let down

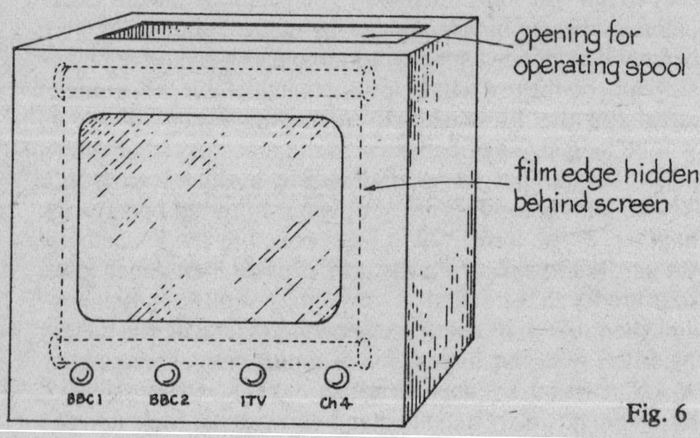

Fig. 6

and hauled up just like a roller blind. No handles or cords are required; the same fingers that activate the puppets can twiddle the roller to raise or lower the 'curtain' as required.

Puppets
Glove puppets can be made very quickly and simply from old discarded gloves and mittens. The thumb and little finger of a glove become the arms, while the three middle fingers are opened out and stitched together into a rounded shape and stuffed to form the head. Features are then painted or embroidered, or appliquéd, on the head, and wool sewn on for hair or beard, or a hat made from scraps of material to form the headgear worn by Punch, a clown, a court jester, a gnome or whatever character is required. If an animal character is required, e.g. Bugs Bunny, the thumb and little finger can form the ears. If desired the hand part of the glove can be embroidered or painted to form a coat or jacket, with buttons sewn on.

Mittens can be cut in such a way that the thumb forms one arm while the other part is shaped to form the head and the other arm. The mitten is then sewn, stuffed and decorated in the same way as a glove.

Finger puppets are usually too big to be easily operable by tiny fingers; these are best left to older children of school age who will make and use them in sizes to fit their hands for the purpose of mime, drama and craftwork in the junior and lower senior classes.

Fig. 7 shows a few ideas for the decoration of puppets made from gloves and mittens.

While on the subject of dress, don't forget that small children simply love dressing-up games. Every playgroup should have a chest full of discarded garments, hats, shoes, wigs, pieces of veiling and old net curtains 'these make terrific bridal outfits!) old blankets (these can be cut into ponchos for aspiring cowboys), handbags, stockings and socks, ties, etc. A tin of black poster paint was kept in one playgroup I visited for use as moustaches and other face make-up. It was not very popular with the parents

who had to scrub it off afterwards, but it was a huge success with the toddlers, who seemed to enjoy painting their friends better than wearing the 'stage make-up' themselves! I asked the playgroup leader why she did not have lipsticks, rouge and powder for little girls who wanted to become 'film stars.' Her reply was that it would put ideas into the children's heads and they would raid their mothers' make-up stocks are home when they were not looking!

Wood offcuts

If you have some wood offcuts, saw these up into small pieces of different sizes and shapes, and carefully sand-paper all the rough edges. Hey presto, you have free building blocks! Children will play happily for hours with the natural wood blocks, but if you want to colour some of them use natural vegetable dyes and not ordinary paint, which could be poisonous if licked.

If you have some flat sheets of thin wood, paste attractive pictures on one side, varnish and leave to dry, then cut up into small pieces of various sizes and shapes. These make absorbing jigsaw puzzles for small hands. Avoid lots of squiggly shapes, which may be very good in a 1000-piece jigsaw for adults but will fox the playgroup set completely! If a child can't make the pieces fit, at this age he is more than likely to fling them on the floor in disgust and turn to something else he *can* do. The concept of overcoming a challenge is not really developed at this age. For the same reason, do not paste a picture on each side of one piece of wood – it will only confuse what is still, after all, a baby mind. And don't forget – when cutting the wood, be sure to smooth all rough edges with sandpaper.

Peg people

Wooden dolly pegs can be cut across the bottom so that they will stand upright, and then painted with various features and clothed with odd scraps of paper or material. They will make whole families (the children are cut shorter), soldiers, policemen, railway porters, bus drivers and conductors, firemen – whatever the children think of. And of course it is they who can paint and dress them, which will keep the kiddies quiet while the harassed playgroup leader does the books or whatever!

Woolly balls

These are for the babies. You just cut two circles of roughly the size you want the finished ball to be, from a piece of cardboard. The two circles must be identical. Then cut a hole in the middle, from one to two inches in diameter according to the size of the ball. Through this hole, using a large darning-needle or bodkin, just keep on threading the wool through, joining any loose pieces, until you have wound on so much wool that you can no longer push the darner easily through the hole.

Now pass a piece of thin string or strong thread through a gap between the two cardboard circles made by snipping through the wool at the outer edges, and knot firmly. This stops the ball unravelling. Remove the cardboard circles, and you now have a woolly ball to dangle from a cot or pram. With a crochet hook make a length of chain, and finish with a loop to hang it by, stitching the other end firmly to the centre of the ball.

This is a good way to use odd bits of wool left over from knitting jobs, as it produces an attractive multicolour effect. Of course, there's nothing to stop you using wool all of the same colour to match baby's cot-cover, but it will be all the same to baby whichever you do.

Keeping the quieter child occupied
A few children prefer solitary pursuits to the rough-and-tumble preferred by the more extrovert members of the playgroup. It is much better to provide such children with an absorbing occupation which they can do by themselves or with just one or two companions, rather than trying to get them to join in noisy or energetic play which they do not feel ready for. The shyer type of child will often prefer to sit at a table drawing and painting, or cutting out and pasting. Here are some ideas for these children.

Save all suitable magazines and coloured pictures, and also brown wrapping paper. Cut the latter into large sheets which can be doubled over to form a large book when several of such doubled sheets are placed together, one inside another. Do not use staples to join them as the sharp points can come adrift; instead sew them with strong thread. Blunt-pointed scissors are used to cut out figures, horses, dogs, etc. from the magazines; these are then pasted into the scrapbooks to form pictures. Ordinary flour-and-water paste is perfectly adequate for this purpose. Its adhesive qualities are enhanced by mixing the flour with water in which rice or potatoes (i.e., starch) have been boiled. The water must be quite cold when used to make the paste. Cheap brushes are the least messy way to use the paste for affixing the pictures.

Other children may like to trace pictures for drawing. Ordinary greaseproof paper can be used – there is no need at all to purchase tracing pads, which are better left to college students. It can be ironed out flat if necessary, just as you can do with used parcel wrapping paper to avoid buying new (e.g. for making the scrapbooks referred to earlier). Make the greaseproof paper into little individual tracing books if you like, or just place one sheet with each drawing, photograph or picture to be traced.

Finally, a diary or project book can be made by cutting sheets of cheap newsprint or lining-paper, or even plain shelf-paper, folding them over and sewing into books as already described. Each child is given a book and some coloured felt-tip pens, and encouraged to draw his or her impressions of the day's events, objects seen in the street or garden, etc. Many a child has started a lifetime habit of keeping a nature diary or observation log from just such small beginnings.

Chapter Seven

The Wardrobe

The best way to save on clothing, said a wit, is to go naked. It's rather akin to the best way to save on the expenses of running a car – just don't buy a car. However, if you have no car you can go by bus, tube, train or even Shanks's pony, but going naked is hardly practicable in our climate. Even nudists wrap up against our winter winds.

Still, it is possible to save quite a lot of money on clothing by being sensible and looking for acceptable alternatives such as making one's own clothes (this saves a bomb), recycling old clothes into new ones by the use of adroit adaptations, finding jumble sale bargains and in some cases remaking them into other items, and so on. Making your own clothes is great fun if you enjoy sewing; it is essential if you are an awkward size and cannot get the garments you want in the material of your choice in your size. I am always amazed at the number of shops that still do not stock anything bigger than a size 18, or even 16! 'What do you think we are,' I asked the manager of one big chain store, 'a nation of midgets?'

The first and most important thing is to take care of the clothes you have. None of this throwing your coat over the back of a chair, or hanging it on a peg without using the loop; this latter treatment will make it look like the Hunchback of Notre Dame in no time. Are you an inveterate screwer-up of shirts, underwear and socks, just bunging the lot into a drawer? That's a big no-no. Worse still, do you pull shirts over your head without unfastening the buttons, and the sleeves over your wrists without taking out the cuff-links? Do you roll up ties, or, horror of horrors, roll one sock inside the other? If you are guilty of any or all of these things, just admit that these careless habits will shorten the life of your clothes by about half. These days with clothing prices what they are, you need to prolong their life by half, not shorten it.

So learn to take care of your clothes. Brush them and hang them up. Unfasten buttons. Use loops. Sponge out spots with cleaning fluid. Make sure that your children emulate your example. Wash clothes as soon as they are soiled. 'Leaving it one more day' is a sure way of ruining a garment. Grit, dust and grime, when left to become ingrained into a fabric, soon rot the threads.

Wash garments by hand if possible rather than by machine, which is rough on delicate fabrics. Don't snuff out their life at the dry cleaner's.

Your shoes, too, are part of your clothing. Treat them with respect. Never dry wet shoes on the hot pipes, over the boiler or in contact with any other form of direct heat. Stuff wet shoes with newspaper and leave them in a current of air to dry. Change the newspaper when it has absorbed moisture. Shoes can be waterproofed by applying dubbin, worked well into the leather, before applying the usual polish. The life of shoes can be doubled by applying stick-on rubber soles to a new pair before they are worn. When these are worn through the original soles are then in use.

Now for some specifics. Even if you are able to use only a quarter of these tips, you should make appreciable savings in clothing.

Shirt into painter's smock
An old frayed or worn shirt makes a good painter's smock. It can be cut down for a schoolchild. The pieces you cut off should be made into pockets, which will be useful to hold brushes, pencils, rubbers, etc. while the artist is working.

Leg-warmers from old jumpers
Cut off the sleeves from old jumpers. These now become leg-warmers. The cuffs are worn at the ankles. Hem the tops to stop them unravelling.

Whiten children's bobby-sox
If bobby-sox are dingy grey, boil them in water containing
a few slices of lemon. You'll be amazed how white and
bright they'll come up.

Renewing shirt collars and cuffs
When the collars and cuffs of shirts fray, there's no need to
discard the garments. Unpick the collars and cuffs, reverse
them and re-attach. Press well, and no one will be able to
tell the difference.

When trousers are too short
Cut the trousers off at knee-length plus an inch and a half
allowance for turning up a hem. Press well. You now have
a smart pair of shorts for the summer (or any other time).

A new use for sheepskin linings
When discarding a sheepskin-lined garment, bootees,
gloves, etc., cut out insoles from the sheepskin linings to
use inside shoes and slippers for additional warmth.

Strengthening school shirts and blouses
Sew a length of wide tape behind the button panel on
school shirts and blouses. Sew through the buttons again,
just as though you were sewing the buttons on to the
garment, but going right through to the strengthening
tape.

Broken straps on shoulder-bags
Buy a luggage-strap of appropriate length, width and
colour, with an adjusting buckle. Choose leather for
strength, rather than plastic. Attach to the bag in place of
the original strap.

New uses for an old plastic raincoat
Cut off the sleeves and insert elastic at each end to make a
pair of waterproof sleeve protectors for wearing when you
do dirty jobs in house or garden, decorating, etc. Cut a

large oblong out of the back to make a waterproof cot sheet, or a waterproof mat to sit on during a picnic. The grass can be damp even if it does not look it.

Making jeans last longer
Jeans, especially children's, will last longer if you stitch contrasting patches on the parts that take the most wear such as the knees. Or, if you prefer, you can make patches from similar material, but cut into the form of pockets. You can add a zip to close the pocket if you like. Such pockets are useful for odds and ends, and the double thickness of the material at these points will prolong the life of the jeans. When the patches or pockets have worn through, unpick them and the original material underneath will still be as good as new.

That old T-shirt
Is your old T-shirt on its last legs? It's about to peg out – literally! Just sew up the bottom, and hang it on a plastic coathanger. It has now become a handy peg-bag. If you want to keep it hanging out on the line, don't use a wire coathanger or it will rust.

Strengthening darned socks
Cut a patch from an old nylon stocking and lay this under the hole to be darned. Darn in the usual way, taking up the threads from the nylon patch. This will not be visible, but will strengthen the darn considerably.

Aprons from plastic dustbin bags
Cut an apron shape from a heavy-duty black plastic dustbin bag, and attach waist tapes and a head loop of matching tape. Such a waterproof apron may not last as long as the heavier store-bought equivalent, but it will be very useful in the kitchen. When it is worn out, detach the loop and tapes to sew to a new apron.

Aprons from old dresses

Cut down old cotton dresses into aprons. They will not be waterproof but will be useful for jobs that do not involve using water.

Dresses into skirts

Jumble sales are full of floor-length dresses that are too small for anyone but Twiggy. Cut the skirt off at such a level that the hips of the dress fit your waist size, hem, and thread elastic through. The length of the skirt will depend on your waist size, i.e. where you have to cut the skirt of the dress. According to your size, the skirt can be anything from short to mid-length or even longer. And of course if you really are as slender as Twiggy but do not want the dress to wear as a dress, your new skirt can be floor-length!

Keep your offcuts of material

Never throw away any pieces of fabric left over from dressmaking, recycling or adapting old garments, etc. You can use suitable pieces for patchwork, dolls' clothes, tea-cosies, cushion covers, table napkins, etc.

Stuffing from old tights

Old tights and stockings, cut into small pieces, make excellent stuffing for cushions, soft toys, etc. These fillings are very resilient and do not go lumpy like kapok.

Children's pyjamas

When children outgrow their pyjamas, lengthen the legs and the sleeves by adding bands of contrasting material. Move the buttons nearer the edge. If still too tight, add a band of the same material to the button edge and re-sew the buttons to allow more room.

School blouses into fancy blouses

If your teenage daughter has left school and does not like her plain blouses, sew lace edging round the collar and on the upper edges of the cuffs, and down each edge of the button panel. The white blouses can also be dyed if desired. Cold-water dyes are simple to use.

Children's shoe-laces

Lengthen the life of children's shoe-laces by frequently re-threading them and so moving their positions in relation to the holes. Keeping them in the same positions weakens them by chafing in the metal eyelets.

Slips into half-slips

If the top of a slip becomes worn, cut the bottom off at the waist, allowing an inch or so to make a hem. Thread narrow elastic through. Add an edging of lace to the bottom if desired. Both ladies' and children's slips may be made into half-slips in this way.

Loops for hooks

Coats and jackets should always have proper loops for hanging up on hooks. Substitute elastic for material, especially in children's garments. This will then stretch instead of snapping in half when pulled.

Another use for roll-collar jumpers

When the sleeves or body of a roll-collar jumper have 'gone', cut off the worn parts and make either a sleeveless roll-collar jumper to be worn with a cardigan, or a 'dicky' to be worn instead of scarves with a coat. Such a 'dicky' also looks smart worn under a V-necked jumper of contrasting colour.

Bedsocks from old jumpers

The sleeves of old jumpers can be fashioned into bedsocks. The cuffs will fit snugly round the legs, and the other end can be cut in such a shape as to fit the feet, and stitched together.

A tip when knitting jumpers

This tip is especially useful for children's jumpers. Knit two small squares in the same wool and sew each square on the inside of each sleeve at the elbow. This will save much darning later. The double thickness will take most of the wear and tear from school desks.

Briefs from tights
When the legs of tights have laddered, cut them off and hem the cut edges neatly. Stitch in a cotton gusset. You have now made a pair of briefs.

Whitening dingy nylon undies
Add half a teaspoonful of cream of tartar to both the washing and the rinsing water. You will be amazed at the transformation.

When buying new clothes . . .
Don't forget that choosing non-iron, drip-dry materials such as Crimplene halves your work in laundering them, your electricity for ironing or pressing and your money for dry cleaning.

An odd leather glove
If you lose one, or find one, cut it into circles to make leather buttons for coats, jerkins, etc. Just glue to button moulds. When laundering garments with leather buttons, protect these buttons in the wash by covering them with kitchen foil.

Fire-resistant fabrics
Fabrics can be made fire-resistant by soaking in a solution of 1 oz alum to a gallon of water.

From fur coat to rug
An old fur coat can make a good fireside rug. Just cut an oblong out of the back, and sew a hessian backing to the reverse side. Fake fur can also be used, and has the additional advantage that it is washable.

A safety pocket for your beach towel
Fold over one corner of your beach towel, sew along one
edge of the triangle so formed, and sew a zip to fit along
the other edge. This forms a safety pocket for your small
change, spectacles, watch and similar items while you go
for a swim.

Alternating your clothes
Don't wear the same clothes or shoes two days running.
Alternate them and 'rest' the ones worn the previous day.
They will last twice as long. This applies particularly to
outdoor shoes. Save wear and tear on outdoor shoes by
wearing indoor shoes in the house. The lighter weight of
indoor shoes will also rest your feet!

Zip trouble
If a zip sticks, rub it with a graphite lead pencil, and it will
run normally.

Re-using knitted garments
When hand-knitted garments can no longer be worn,
unpick and wind off the wool. To get all the crinkles out,
wash the skeins of wool in soap flakes, rinse thoroughly,
and hang up to dry without squeezing. The wool will come
up like new, and you can knit a new garment.

Talking of knitting . . .
Wool is much cheaper if bought in bulk from mail order
firms in the spinning towns of the North. They usually
have a very good choice and can send you a catalogue with
samples of the actual wool, usually free.

Hairdressing for the family
Learn to cut, style and set your own and your family's
hair. Why pay inflated prices to a hairdresser for shampoo,
setting lotion, etc.? The first time you may end up looking
like Harpo Marx, but after a few attempts you soon get the
hang of it. The simpler the style, the easier it is to do. If

you must have a perm, get a friend to give you a home perm.

A button jar
Save all buttons from discarded garments and keep them in a jar. They may come in useful when making new garments or adapting others. Complete sets of buttons will save you money as the cost of new buttons to-day is out of all proportion to their intrinsic value. One button as a replacement for one that has been lost is also a money-saver, since you do not then need to buy a whole set just for one button. Buttons can also be covered with material to match the garment they are to fasten. They also make cuff-links if they are good enough. Just join in pairs with a shank between. To make the shank, leave an inch of thread between the buttons as you join them, then blanket-stitch over these threads to make them into one strong connecting-link.

Sometimes jumble sale dresses, blouses, coats, etc. may be too grotty to wear but have marvellous sets of buttons. It is then worth paying the few pence for the garment just to get the buttons. The same goes for zips, insets of embroidery, lace insertion, etc. Keep a lookout for the older garments as these often have real mother-of-pearl buttons instead of cheap plastic imitations.

When you have to buy a set of buttons for a new garment you are making, buy one or two more than you need, so that should one fall off and get lost you will not need to buy a whole set in order to replace the missing button.

Hankies galore
Cut squares from discarded cotton dresses and hem all round to make new handkerchiefs. Squares cut from plain material can be embroidered in one corner with an initial or a floral motif. The cheapest place to find embroidery transfers is on the antique bric-à-brac market stall. Look for old pattern books and women's magazines. Paper patterns often find their way to these stalls, too, at two or

three pence each instead of the £1.50 or more you would have to pay in the shops.

Save on tights

Buy tights in the same colour, two pairs or more at a time, so that when one leg ladders in each of two pairs you can cut off the laddered legs and wear the two pairs together, thus forming one new pair with a double brief. See page 000 for what to do when *both* legs of one pair of tights ladder.

If the laddered legs you have cut off are not yet bad enough to use as polishing pads or to stuff cushions, cut them off at knee level and turn in a small neat hem. Thread through with dirndl elastic, and they will make knee-high socks to wear under jeans.

Half-slips from old dresses

The skirt of an old cotton summer dress that has seen better days can still make a useful half-slip. Hem the top and elasticate it, and if desired add lace edging to the bottom. Buy lace on market stalls, on which it is a few pence a yard, vastly cheaper than the department-store equivalent.

Brightening up a plain jumper or cardigan

Embroider some simple floral design in contrasting wools on an old plain jumper or cardigan. This will give it a new lease of life. Any weak spots can have the embroidery strategically placed over them. You could also knit a new collar and cuffs in a contrasting colour if you liked. You would feel that you had a new jumper!

New jumpers from old

See page 000 on how to unravel old hand-knitted jumpers to re-knit into new ones. Then look out for hand-knitted jumpers at jumble sales and recycle them. One ladies' or men's jumper or cardigan will make up into two children's garments. Any left-over wool could be knitted into men's ties, which look very smart with suitable 'tweedy' suits and jackets.

Another use for old jumpers

Machine-made or synthetic jumpers can be re-cut to make warm winter dresses for little girls. Without sleeves, they make good pinafore dresses to wear over the child's existing jumpers or blouses. Make a deep hem so that the dress can be lengthened and thus give more wear as the child grows taller.

Knitting children's jumpers

When knitting the sleeves, start at the shoulder edge and end with the cuffs, Then, as the child grows and the sleeves become too short, it is a simple matter to unpick the cuffs, pick up the stitches and knit the sleeves longer. To prepare for this, you must, of course, be sure to have enough wool left over after the original knitting.

Babies' rompers

When baby outgrows a romper, cut off the bottom and make a hem. This will now make a dress for a girl or a shirt for a boy, as the baby grows bigger.

School notice boards

Watch the school notice boards for used bargains in school uniforms, often in very good condition, being outgrown long before outworn. A notice board is often displayed in some clinics, PTA meeting-rooms, church halls, etc. and similar bargains may be found 'on the cards'.

Knee and elbow patches

Leather offcuts can often be picked up cheaply by the bag from shoe repairers, handbag-manufacturers, and so on. These bags, usually available for only a few pence, frequently contain sizeable pieces. They are useful for making elbow and knee patches to sew on to coats, jeans, jackets, etc. to strengthen them at the points where they receive the most wear. They are also useful for mending the uppers of shoes and slippers that have worn through, and for making sandals.

Teach your children to knit, crochet and sew
These skills, like the ability to cook, are invaluable assets to a child on growing to adulthood. Lay the foundations while the children are small. They can knit squares to make up into blankets for their own rooms, as no fancy patterns are required and the squares do not require discouragingly large numbers of stitches to be cast on. The thicker the wool used, the fewer the stitches (and the warmer the blanket). The decorative patchwork blanket can be used as a bedcover. Both boys and girls should be able to sew on buttons, darn socks and mend torn clothes. A bachelor's apartment does not have to look like a male chauvinist pig-sty.

New life for an old cardigan
Cut off the sleeves and bind the armholes with contrasting bias binding. Bind the edges of the neck and front fastening edges with the same material. This makes an attractive jerkin which can be worn over a blouse or jumper. If the cardigan has pockets, bind the top edge of each pocket with the tape to match.

Hairdressing for free
If you're not too fussy about having a particular hair style, some ladies' salons have 'student evenings' when they will give a free shampoo, cut and styling on the understanding that the girl (or boy) who is a learner is free to cut and style your hair in the way the salon wishes her/him to learn the job. Some salons call these 'model evenings' and the hapless victims 'models'. There is some supervision though, so you will not come out with your hair dyed green or styled like a punk rocker.

You will see from all the above hints that it's quite possible to clothe oneself adequately and even attractively at minimal cost. Who needs to go naked?

Chapter Eight

Christmas, Birthday and Gift Time

Lots of savings can be effected here. One of the best is to haunt the sales (usually January and July) and snap up attractive items to keep for use as gifts when occasion demands, such as at Christmas and for birthdays, anniversaries and so on. The same items on sale at Christmas time, for example, will have rocketed in price because the wily shopkeepers know that people will be looking for them. Your saving is effected because you buy the item as a time of low demand and the price is accordingly reduced.

Christmas wrapping paper

If in good condition, not torn and not written upon, this can be ironed out flat on the reverse side and re-used. If it is a good-quality paper it will come up like new.

If it is not in quite such pristine condition, staple sheets together to make disposable tablecloths, either for children's parties, or for picnics.

Old Christmas cards

Use the best ones to make calendars. Cut off the message part, leaving the picture, and mount on a larger sheet of white or coloured card. Attach a calendar, and a loop at the top to hang it up.

Very large Christmas cards can also be made into desk blotters. Cut the blotting to fit and staple it to the fold of the card. Cards in smaller sizes might be usefully made into blotters for children to use in school.

Another use for old Christmas cards is to make gift tags. Cut all round the picture with pinking shears and punch two small holes along one of the shorter edges for the ribbon to tie.

Christmas decorations

Many things can be pressed into service to make your own Christmas decorations. Collect twigs, cones, etc. and spray them with gold or silver paint, or with imitation spray-on 'snow'. Save the wishbones from chickens and turkeys and, after washing well, paint these in similar fashion. Cut imitation mistletoe and holly leaves from green paper and make 'berries' by attaching red or white beads with pins, and create a border for a bulletin board by pinning these along the edges. Paint peanuts (in their shells) gold or silver and thread them on lengths of cotton with a large darning-needle, and hang them over the branches of the Christmas tree.

Make your own 'icicles'. Dissolve 3 oz powdered alum in a pint of boiling water, then dip pieces of string into it. Leave some of the pieces in the solution longer than others, to vary the thickness of the finished icicles. Hang up to dry before use.

Cake decorating

Save the caps from washing-up liquid containers. These can be turned into miniature Christmas-tree tubs. Fill with plasticine, then stick a sprig of an evergreen tree into it to form the Christmas tree. Arrange on top of the cake.

You do not need to buy a cake frill. Cut a strip of kitchen foil the width and length required, and stitch along the centre a wide satin ribbon, piece of lace or strip of ruched chiffon fabric. Cut the sides of the foil strip into narrow strips to a depth of about half an inch on each side. Attach to the cake, joining the overlapped ends with Sellotape. Do not be tempted to stick pins into the cake to fix it – this is dangerous.

The Christmas tree

Don't buy a cut-off tree wedged in a tub. This will die, shedding its needles all over the carpet to jam up your hoover. Buy a *live* tree in a tub of soil. This will last years if watered just like any other plant. If you have a garden put it outside all year and just bring it in for Christmas. It will, of course, grow a little each year.

If you have little room and would find a growing tree a problem, buy a good imitation tree. This will last indefinitely and will not drop any litter.

Never use candles to light a Christmas tree, however tempted you may be. One has only to knock the tree, or a gust of wind blow on it from a window, and the whole lot can go up, with disastrous results. A set' of electric Christmas-tree lights should be used if you wish to have a lighted tree, but these must be checked by a competent electrician. After switching on the tree lights fixed by an amateur electrician, I have personally known of three instances in which fuses blew out as soon as this was done. In one particular case the fuses of the entire flat blew out, leaving the Christmas revellers in darkness. 'Oh, what fun!' cried the children as they groped about with torches – until they found that the TV would not work and they had to miss their favourite programme.

Some novel children's gifts
A dolls' bunk bed can be made from two stacking plastic vegetable racks. Slot them together and make mattresses to fit from pieces of foam rubber. A large-size budgerigar's ladder can lead to the top bunk (two joined together if one is not long enough). Make sheets, pillow-cases and bedspreads from pieces of scrap material from your rag-bag. Printed cotton can be used for the top sheets, a toning darker shade of plain cotton for the bottom sheets and pillow-cases, and the bedspreads can be made in patchwork from smaller pieces.

Those boxes of dates which are oblong with rounded ends make very good pencil-cases after the dates have been enjoyed. Wash out thoroughly to remove any trace of stickiness, and wash off the label. Cover with stick-on Fablon and line with either the same material or with soft fabric glued into place. The child's name, address and the school form number can be attached in Dynotape.

A brand-new jigsaw puzzle can be made from an old one

on which the picture has faded or rubbed off, provided that all the pieces are intact with none missing. Find a suitable picture of the exact size to fit, and glue it over the made-up puzzle. When the glue has dried, cut through the edges of the puzzle pieces with the point of a Stanley knife. Hey presto – you have a new puzzle.

Make a draughtboard. You need a piece of flat wood for the board, and enough black and white vinyl stick-on tiles to cover it when the tiles are cut into 1½-inch squares. Stick these on, alternating black with white, to form a checkerboard surface. Now take a piece of one-inch dowel rod and saw this into rounds half an inch thick. Sandpaper the edges. These form the counters. Paint them in two different colours, or paint half of them and leave the other half plain and unpainted. Alternatively, bottle-tops may be used, similarly painted. Glue two tops together to make each counter, to avoid injury from the pointed 'teeth' on the underside of the bottle-top.

Save unwanted embroidery transfers and iron these on to sheets of lining paper. Staple or sew these together to form a book. This makes a painting book.

A pencil or crayon holder for school or home use can be made by cutting an empty washing-up liquid container in half. Paint the bottom half a bright colour and stencil a design on it – the child's name, perhaps. Don't throw away the top half – it will make a useful funnel for the kitchen! (after you have removed the cap, of course).

The young potter can model in 'clay' made by mixing three parts flour and one part salt with one part cold water. Stir well, and divide this 'clay' into several batches, each coloured with a different vegetable food colouring. After the models have been made, they may be baked hard in the oven.

A cheap and safe glue for children to use may be made by mixing flour and cold water to make creamy paste. The child can make his or her own scrapbook by pasting in newspaper and magazine cuttings, comic cartoons, nature pictures, football star cards, etc, after making the book itself from brown wrapping paper stapled or sewn together to form the pages of a book.'

Notelets may be made by folding ordinary white typing paper in four and pasting a coloured cut-out picture on the front, or painting a design if art is your *forte*. You can also make children's notepaper by sticking a small motif on to the top heft-hand corner of the paper or, again, if preferred, you can paint a design. The same design could be painted on the flap of the envelope to make a matching set.

If your children are at all artistic, encourage them to draw and paint their own Christmas, birthday and other greeting cards. These will be original and personal. They can also compose their own poems for the verses inside the card.

Posters for teenagers' rooms can often be obtained free from travel bureaux when they are going to replace them with updated versions. It costs nothing to ask. Sometimes sheets of giftwrap contain not an all-over design but just one complete picture. This is often attractive enough to form a wall poster, at minimal cost.

Foster a love of music in your children. I don't mean just listening to music, good though this is, but *making* music. Bamboo pipes, recorders, etc. are not outrageously expensive. If you have a piano, so much the better. A few children could form their own group and meet regularly to play or even compose their own music. And don't forget the musical instrument that costs nothing – the human voice.

Chapter Nine

Paper

Paper is one of the commodities on which you can save quite a lot, as it is so versatile. Odd scrap paper, brochures, leaflets, old envelopes, newspapers and magazines, paper bags, brown parcel-wrapping paper – all these can be used and re-used for many things after their original function has ended. Even cereal packets need not go into the dustbin.

Let us now take a look at the ways in which you can save on paper. (Things to do with paper which will effect savings on fuel are dealt with in Chapter Eleven).

Re-use cardboard packets

Save all the cardboard packets and boxes in which foodstuffs and kitchen equipment, soaps, detergents, etc. are packed. Cut into strips and keep them in a jam-jar by the cooker for use as tapers for lighting one gas jet from another.

Perhaps you cook by electricity, in which case you may prefer to cut the cardboard into small oblongs to use as shopping lists, notes to put out for the milkman, etc.

If you have children, they will enjoy cutting out the cartoon animal faces and other figures from cereal packets and other food cartons to paste into their scrapbooks, or to make into stand-up figures to play with by pasting tabs on the back. Or they may like to use them to play shops with. I always remember a girl who went to the same junior school as myself, whose father had a disused garden shed. He rigged this up with lots of shelves and a counter, and my school chum and her friends all collected empty packets to use for their 'stock'. They even clubbed together to save up for a good working toy cash register. I used to enjoy these Saturday-afternoons when about four or five of us would take it in turns to be the shopkeeper or the customers. No VAT inspectors in those days . . . nor did we need to chain and padlock our bicycles outside!

Waxed paper box linings
The waxed paper bags which line cereal boxes should be opened out flat and circles cut out of them for your jam-making sessions. (See Chapter Ten for how to make the transparent film outer circles for free).

Newspaper as underlay
Newspaper make a perfectly good underlay for a carpet. They have the added advantage of being very good for insulation and thus will help conserve heat. Make pads from newspaper to lay under the treads of a stair carpet. These reduce wear, and so will make the carpet last longer. When pressure of use has worn the newspaper pads thin, replace them.

Butter and margarine wrappers
Store these, greased side inwards when folded, in a plastic bag to use for greasing cake and flan tins.

Plain-backed printed circulars
These can be cut into oblongs for use as shopping lists and notes for the milkman or other tradesmen.

Scrapbooks for children(and adults)
Make a scrapbook from brown parcel-wrapping paper, sewing or stapling the pages together. After reading magazines and newspapers, cut out any items of interest for pasting into the scrapbooks. Children and teenagers may like to cut out pictures of film and TV stars, footballers, rock and pop groups and news items connected with these. Adults may like to save recipes, embroidery, knitting, crochet and dressmaking patterns, articles on health and child care, slimming exercises and diets, etc. Both adults and children may like to save nature pictures and articles.

Old magazines

If these have not had bits cut out of them, give them to hospitals, ladies' hairdressers or your doctor's waiting-room. Children's comics will also be appreciated by hospitals and doctors but I doubt that the ladies under the drier at the local salon would care for them very much.

Greaseproof paper from bread

The greaseproof paper from certain kinds of wrapped sliced bread can be re-used in many ways, such as lining cake tins, covering cakes during baking, wrapping sandwiches for lunch-packets, and as a base for piping cake decorations in icing sugar intended for storing. The waxed paper from cereal packets can also be used in these ways.

Brown paper bags for the Hoover

The heavy-duty brown paper bags given away by Safeways and other supermarkets are the exact size of the standard dust-bag in the domestic Hoover. The advantage of using them is that when they are filled with dust they can just be detached and destroyed, and a new one attached in its place. Much better and more hygienic than scrabbling about in a linen bag full of fluff and stuff.

Pedal bin liners

You need never buy them. I have not bought them for years. Just use the plastic carrier bags you use for shopping when a handle goes or a seam splits. Large plastic bags (see next chapter) can also be used.

Cardboard rolls from kitchen towels and foil

These make absolutely super postal rolls for sending printed matter through the mails, as they are virtually crush-proof and do not weigh as much as the specially-manufactured article sold in stationery shops, so they save you money on postage, too.

Cardboard rolls from toilet-rolls

These vary in strength but they are not long enough to use as postal rolls; however, the stronger ones can be cut into 1½-inch rings and covered with Fablon or other decoration for use as table napkin rings. There's a job that will keep the children occupied for a bit. Model-makers can also use them for ships' funnels, engine funnels, etc. They can be cut down to size if too big.

Another use for long cardboard tubes

The central roll from kitchen towels or foil can also be used to form the basis of a draught-excluder to put at the bottom of a door. Pad it all round with plastic foam padding and cover it with a remnant of material. You now have a 'sausage-dog' to keep the wind out and the warmth in.

Magazine cut-out cookery pictures

These will brighten up a dull kitchen no end if pasted on the insides of doors, cupboards, etc., or even on the walls. Anyone who sees them will probably think you cook these exotic gourmet dishes all the time! What I like about this idea, though, is that you can enjoy the sight of all that glorious food without putting on a single calorie!

Used wrapping paper

You can re-use this if you iron it out flat again with a warm iron. Sellotape stuck to it will come off quite easily if you run the iron over it. If it leaves a mark, this can be covered by an address label or a 'Fragile' label on the parcel.

Re-use of envelopes

Re-use envelopes by sticking an address label over the old address and re-sealing with Sellotape. Large manila envelopes can be re-used again and again in this way. Avoid confusion by removing or covering the old used stamps before affixing the new ones.

Bookmarks from cardboard
Strips of cardboard can be cut from food packets to make bookmarks. Cover with oddments of fabric, wallpaper, or a 'collage' made up of colourful magazine pictures, pasted on to the cardboard backing.

Notelets made at home
Ordinary typing paper, folded in four, can be decorated on the top outer fold with a pasted-on cut-out picture, or with a painting of your own design if you are artistic. Stencils may also be used.

TV and radio programmes
The times for these, with brief details, are printed in all daily newspapers. It's cheaper to buy a daily newspaper than to take the *TV Times* and *Radio Times*. All the Sunday programmes are given in the Saturday newspaper. With the daily paper you have all the news – which of course is not covered by the two weeklies.

Old magazines and comics
Subscription magazines often have a secondhand value, so save them. Complete sets are often in demand on the secondhand market even only a year or two after the end of the run. Stockpile children's comics until they have forgotten the contents. Then bring them out again if the children have to stay in bed with illness. They will be appreciated as much as new ones.

Cover your cookbooks
Make covers for your cookbooks just like we used to have to make covers for our school books when we were at school, to keep them clean. A cover on your cookbook may not look so good but it will stop it from acquiring greasy thumbprints. You can use transparent paper to make the cover if you prefer, instead of brown paper, wallpaper, giftwrap paper or suchlike.

Protection in a cardboard box

Find a cardboard carton at the supermarket which is just marginally taller, when stood on one end or on its side, than a milk bottle. Then put this out for the milkman to stand your milk bottles in. This will effectively stop the tom-tits from pecking through your milk bottle tops to get at the cream. No lid is required, as the birds will not go into a dark box.

Another use for large brown paper bags

Open them out to make into sheets of brown paper for wrapping small parcels. These bags are usually very strong.

Self-adhesive labels

These, cut into narrow strips, can be used to make alterations to address books and telephone number notebooks. These are much neater than crossing out and scribbling over the original entries, as well as being much clearer to read.

Waxed paper for the freezer

The waxed paper from cereal packets is very good for layering foods for the freezer. Cut into pieces the size of the freezing containers for layering bacon, meat, lemon slices, layers of sponge cake for gateaux, rolled-out pastry, etc.

Cage bird floors

Instead of the expensive sanded sheets, use ordinary newspaper cut to fit the bottom of the cage. Put several layers at a time on the floor of the cage, and remove the top one every day. This keeps the cage clean and hygienic and costs nothing, as you buy the newspapers to read anyway.

Paper for an emergency

I refer, of course, to paper *money*! Keep a pound note in a sealed envelope hidden in the deepest recesses of your handbag, or in a pocket of an outdoor garment. If you run out of money, or mislay your wallet or purse, you will not be stranded as you will at least have your fare to get home.

Chapter Ten

Forty Ways of Re-Using Plastic Bags

1   Wrap packed lunches for schoolchildren, working men, picnics, etc. first in grease-proof paper and then in a plastic bag. This protects the food from dust, etc. and also protects the clothing, pocket, satchel or brief-case from grease.

2   On picnics, the same plastic bags that contained sandwiches, salads or other foods can be used to transport litter home if there are no waste-bins available. They can also be used to bring home the used cutlery, plates and dishes if you are not using disposables.

3   For those who are, like myself, naturalists, a supply of plastic bags in various sizes is indispensable for bringing home one's specimens, especially aquatic material, mosses, plant specimens, and so on. They make excellent miniature 'ponds' for children to bring home or take to school tadpoles, frog-spawn, minnows or sticklebacks, pondweed, caddis-worms, dragon-fly larvae, water-beetles, water-boatmen, etc. for the aquarium. For botanists the plastic bag has entirely superseded the clumsy, heavy old-fashioned vasculum. The empty bags take up no space at all to speak of, and when botanical specimens are put into them they are kept separated and not jammed together as they used to be in a vasculum, inevitably damaging and wilting them.

4   Jam and preserve makers will find plastic bags invaluable. To make the circles to cover the tops, just cut circles out of the bags to the correct sizes. When making pickles containing vinegar, if you have no plastic, glass or rubber closures, you can in an emergency press metal lids into service by covering

the jar first with a double thickness of plastic bag cut to size, to prevent the vinegar from touching the metal of the lid and setting up harmful chemical changes.

5 Protect your library book when it is raining by slipping it into a plastic bag. If you carry your book under your arm, it will also protect your clothing from being irreparably stained by the dyes which are frequently used in the binding of library books. The red covers seem to be the worst.

6 The cost of expensive propagator-tops for seedlings can be entirely eliminated by using plastic bags in the manner described in Chapter Thirteen on gardening.

7 If you have no trays or saucers to put under your indoor plant pots, a plastic bag covered by a kitchen paper towel makes a good mat to put under the pot. The plastic bag will prevent moisture from staining the window-ledge or other surface on which the pot stands, and the paper towel (folded four times) will absorb the water when you water the plant and prevent the surplus from running over the edge of the bag.

If you have a large number of pot plants standing in rows on window-ledges, as I have (I specialize in bromeliads and aroid plants) you will find that a large black plastic rubbish-bag, folded lengthwise until you have made it the width of the ledge, will be very effective. Nothing, but nothing, ruins the paintwork of window-ledges as surely as diluted fertilizer running out of the bottoms of plant pots. *Experto crede*!

8 These bags are very useful in the kitchen. To coat chicken joints, fish, etc. with seasoned flour, put enough flour, salt and pepper into the bag, shake together, then put in the joint or fish and shake until thoroughly coated. This avoids your getting your hands (and the floor) covered with flour. You can also crush digestive biscuits inside a plastic bag with a rolling-pin to make graham crumbs for cheesecakes. The same goes for crushing granulated sugar to make

castor sugar. With a brown paper bag you cannot see when the crumbs or the sugar are fine enough. This method is just as good as using a blender, and you don't have to wash out the blender afterwards.

9　When travelling, put bottles of shampoo or other containers of liquid into plastic bags, as a safety precaution just in case the caps come off, or pressure of other luggage on top of your case bursts the containers. Your clothes will then be saved from being stained with the liquids.

10　Travelling again, take a wet flannel in a plastic bag for wiping hands after eating a picnic, wiping children's sticky fingers and faces, or simply for dabbing on one's brow when it's stiflingly hot in the car.

11　When camping, keep matches in a plastic bag to stop damp getting into them.

12　Protect the pages of your cookbook when referring to it in a steamy kitchen by covering them with a plastic bag. Better still, put the whole book, opened, into the bag. A still better idea is to look to the ventilation and not have a steamy kitchen in the first place.

13　Hang a number of hand-size plastic bags on a nail or hook in the wall of the coal-hole. Use them as disposable 'gloves' when sorting lumps of coal to put into your coal-scuttle.

14　If you have a dirty job to do in the kitchen or garden, cut the bottoms off two plastic bags, put your hands through them and fasten them over the ends of your sleeves with rubber bands to protect your sleeves.

15　If you have a wooden clothes-horse, prevent wood-stains on the clothes by laying plastic bags on the rails first before hanging the clothes on them.

16　May your holiday snapshots and postcards into colourful tablemats. Glue them on to cork tiles, then cover the decorated side with an opened-out plastic bag, securing it on the reverse side with glue or Sellotape, for protection.

17 A large plastic bag makes a good hairdo-protector to wear in the bath or shower. Make a circle of elastic with which to keep the bag firmly on your head.

18 Take your own bags to market, as many market stallholders do not provide them, or else they wrap vegetables in newspaper, which comes apart so that potatoes, etc. spill soil out into your carrier bag or shopping basket. Plastic bags are stronger than brown paper bags.

19 Take a plastic bag with you when eating out. In America, restaurants provide 'doggy bags' for leftovers which are good enough to take home. After all, you have paid for the food, so you are entitled to it. If a restaurant gives you a huge portion which you cannot manage, you should have no qualms about putting the unused portion unobtrusively into your plastic bag to take home. It is absolutely wrong to waste food when there are so many people in the world who never have enough to eat. It is time that restaurateurs in this country followed the American example, but until such time as they do, take your own bag.

20 Take large plastic bags in car journeys with a baby so that the soiled nappies can be placed in them – the terries to be taken home and the disposables to be taken to the nearest public toilet.

21 Large plastic bags can be used as pedal bin liners. If you do not use a pedal bin but take rubbish direct to an outside dustbin, wrap rubbish in plastic bags first to avoid soiling the bin with messy kitchen waste. When such waste is wrapped in newspaper, liquids often seep through and leave soggy messes in the dustbin. The most hygienic method is to use a large black plastic dustbin liner first in any case and then put the rubbish in wrapped individually as described above.

22 It is cheaper to buy a large sliced loaf, but unless you have a big family it tends to last longer than you would like it to from the viewpoint of staying fresh.

Cut the loaf in half, and freeze one half, wrapped in a plastic bag, in your freezer or in the freezing compartment of your fridge. It will stay fresh until when you want to use it. Take it out two or three hours beforehand to thaw out.

23   If you have a large family of biscuit-eating children and keep a tin of biscuits, this soon contains a number of broken biscuits caused by all the delving into the tin. These broken pieces are usually carefully avoided by the delvers! Pack all these broken biscuits into little plastic bags and seal the top edges to make 'Snack packs' to take to football matches, walking and cycling expeditions and so on when the children will be much less fussy! To seal the top edges in a professional-looking manner (as opposed to merely using a wire closure), lay the two edges together inside a folded length of kitchen foil, and run a warm iron over the foil. The heat seals the plastic by fusing it together, but does not affect the strip of foil, which is simply peeled off for re-use. Your children will think you are very clever when they see the sealed bags – just like the commercial ones from the supermarket!

24   Plastic bags can be used to cover open tubs or jars of food in the fridge which have no lids. Just slip a rubber band over the top to keep them in place. They can be re-used again and again, except when they have been used for fish, garlic or other strong-smelling foods.

25   Strong plastic bags can be used as freezer containers, but the very thin ones are unsuitable for this use.

26   Butter and margarine papers, kept for greasing and lining cake tins or for covering cakes, roast joints, etc., should be stored in a plastic bag in the fridge. The bag stops the butter or margarine from hardening.

27   Use plastic bags to line waste-paper baskets in living-rooms, bedrooms and so on. Then all you have to do is to lift out the bags, complete with the rubbish, for immediate hygienic disposal.

28 To keep a chamois leather window-cloth soft and ready for use, wash in soapy water and rinse well after use, squeeze lightly, and store in a plastic bag.

29 One can never have enough ice-cubes in the fridge during the summer months. When the cubes in the freezer trays have frozen, take them out instead of leaving them in the trays, and store in plastic bags. Then you can freeze more water in the ice-cube trays.

30 When you go out to buy fish and chips take a large plastic bag with you. Put your fish and chips in this. The combined action of newspaper insulation and the plastic bag will keep the fish and chips far hotter than newspaper alone would do, so you save both time and gas as you will not need to re-heat them on your return home.

31 When freezing a casserole or other dish in the oven-ware in which it has been cooked, after cooling, line the dish or casserole first with a plastic bag and then pour in the food. After freezing all you have to do is to lift the bag containing the food out of the dish. This releases the dish for you to use for cooking, and the frozen dish is the right shape to fit into it again when you are ready to thaw and serve it, or re-heat it, in the same dish. Of course it goes without saying that you must not line the oven dish with plastic *before* cooking, or *before* re-heating! The easiest method is to pour the food into a large bowl or saucepan after cooking and allow it to cool in that, then put the bag into the original cooking-dish and pour the food back again before putting it into the freezer. To re-heat, lift out the bag containing the frozen food, peel off the bag and put the frozen food back into the dish. It will fit exactly!

32 Use large plastic bags for the storage of clothes put away for the summer or winter. Don't forget moth-balls with the woollens, blankets and quilts, and don't store *any* linen or clothing for long periods in an airing cupboard, as this will soon discolour fabrics, especially whites, which turn a dingy yellow.

33 Keep a plastic bag over the head of your squeezy sponge mop after use. This will prevent it from drying out and cracking, and will add months to the life of the sponge.

34 Keep washed lettuce, watercress and parsley in plastic bags in the salad compartment at the bottom of the fridge. The water left after washing should be lightly clinging to the leaves, and the bag should not be closed as this would encourage mould. Kept in this manner the saladings should last several days.

35 Freeze home-made 'ready meals', in individual or family size portions, in ordinary plastic bags. When required for use, remove from the bag and put the food into the special 'boil-in-the-bag' to heat in water. This helps to lengthen the life of the special freezer bags, so that less expenditure will be needed for them.

36 Carry a couple of plastic bags, big enough to cover your shoes with you if you anticipate going into a muddy area, such as into a bog or swamp looking for botanical specimens, gathering wild foods and so on. Cover your shoes with the bags to protect them from the mud and to keep water out. A rubber band or ring of elastic round your ankles will stop the bags from slipping off or getting stuck in the mud.

37 Keep your camera and films in a sealed plastic bag when travelling in hot, moist climates, to avoid mould forming on the moisture-sensitive lens and emulsions.

38 When folding clothes for packing in your luggage, fold them over plastic bags instead of tissue paper, as these are much more springy and help to prevent creases forming. It also helps to fold the clothes widthways instead of lengthways. Any creases will then drop out more easily when the garment is unpacked and hung up.

39 Cut a large plastic bag diagonally from corner to corner after first opening it out flat. Staple or tape two ribbons or lengths of tape to the two long points of the triangle. You now have a handy hood to protect your hair-do from rain after visiting the hairdresser.

40 When painting around doorknobs, sink taps, etc. and
    you don't want to unscrew them and put them back
    again, protect them with plastic bags held on by
    rubber bands, to avoid getting blobs of paint on
    them.

Chapter Eleven

Fuel

In this chapter I am going to include energy-saving and also some tips on saving gas and electricity, as these, too, are derived from solid fuel. After all, not all of us are lucky enough to have an open fire and be able to enjoy the comforting warmth of blazing logs, as opposed to clinical-looking hot pipes. Still fewer of us have that joy of joys, a wood-burning boiler which provides not only warmth but constant hot water and also avoids your needing to cook by gas or electricity. Provided that you can collect and chop your own wood, you can forget all about gas bills, and your electricity bill will be small as it will be covering only lighting and the use of appliances such as TV, hi-fi, electric iron, Hoover and so on. I may be sticking my neck out but I would also go as far as to say that food cooked on a wood-burning stove tastes far better than that cooked in any other way.

Kitchen foil as a reflector

Kitchen foil, being made of aluminium, reflects heat. Paste sheets of foil behind the hot pipes, on top of the wallpaper, and the heat will all go out into the room, not up the wall and out of the window. Put a sheet of foil under the hotplate when you cook by electricity, and this will double the amount of heat going up into the cooking-pot, so that you need a much lower setting. Wrap food in separate small parcels of foil (e.g. vegetables with a little butter) and boil these all in the same pan. This will not only save gas or electricity but the vegetables or other food will be beautifully cooked without being drowned in lots of soggy water which boils out most of their vitamin content.

Tips to save heat when cooking
A metal skewer pushed straight through the potato from end to end when baking potatoes will conduct more heat so that the potato will cook in half the time.

Save any water left after boiling vegetables in the normal way. This contains vitamins from the vegetables. Use it to make the gravy. Being already hot, you will not need to use heat to bring it to the boil.

Turn off the oven ten minutes before the end of cooking time when cooking by electricity. The residual heat will be sufficient to finish cooking the food. Unfortunately this does not seem to work with gas.

When boiling cut potatoes to make mashed or creamed potatoes, cut them into small pieces, which cook much more quickly than large ones.

When cooking on top of the stove always use the smallest ring and the smallest pan you can, and don't let gas flames lick the sides of the pan – the heat required for cooking comes through the bottom of the pan, not the sides, so your food will not be ready any sooner.

Saving on lighting
Fluorescent lighting may well cost less to run in the long term but I would never recommend it for domestic use because it is so bad for the eyes. Just use ordinary bulbs. Use low-wattage bulbs where it is not essential to have a bright light, but do not use them where you need a good light for reading, sewing, etc. Dust all bulbs regularly – it is amazing how much brighter the light is when dust has been removed! Try to avoid very dark shades, as these cut out a lot of the light. And, above all, turn out lights in rooms you are not using.

Don't buy the so-called 'long-life' bulbs. Although these do usually last longer than the standard ones, they also use much more electricity. They therefore increase your electricity bill as well as costing more in the first place anyway.

Saving on coal and coke
Buy your coal and coke at summer prices. The reduction

in price is usually made on fuel purchased between May and September. If you buy large quantities you may also get a discount for spot cash on delivery.

Home-made 'fuels'
Save all newspapers, and when you have enough roll them tightly and fasten with string, wire or strong tape so that they do not unroll. Dip them into water and then squeeze out and leave to dry. These make very good 'logs' to eke out coal and coke. After all, newspaper is made from wood in the first place!

Save all your potato peelings, and leave to dry. They should be packed tightly into paper (not plastic) bags. These will be found to burn very well and save on coal and coke.

Lagging tanks and pipes
Be sure to lag all tanks and pipes which hold hot water. A well-lagged tank will retain heat in the water long after the power has been turned off.

Draught-excluding
Foam draught excluders should be fitted to outside doors all round, not just at the bottom. If you have any gaps between floorboards, lay a sheet of heavy plastic material over the floorboards under the material used as a carpet underlay. Newspapers make very good insulation and if you lay a good thickness of these under the carpet you do not need a felt underlay.

A two-inch layer of glass fibre insulation material laid between the ceiling joists in your loft or attic will reduce heat loss through the roof by up to 75%. The outlay on such roof insulation is an investment which will have paid for itself in about two years by the amount of fuel saved for heating the house.

Washing the dishes
Washing up under a running hot tap is certainly more

hygienic but it does waste a lot of hot water and thus the gas or electricity which heats it. Use a bowl.

Divided cooking-pans

The cooking pans that are divided into two or three compartments to be used on one gas or electric ring are a terrific saving in the heat required for cooking.

Save gas when cooking

If you have to cook food in three or four pans at the same time such as when preparing a full meal for the family, put a square sheet of iron over the top of one gas ring (this is not suitable for electric cookers). Put the pan containing the main item which takes longest to cook over the ring, and light the gas. Put the other pans around it on top of the iron sheet. This very soon becomes as hot as the gas ring and will cook all the pots of food on just the one ring. This is one of the biggest savings for anyone who has to cook large family meals every day on a gas stove.

De-scale kettles regularly

A de-scaled kettle boils water much faster than one which is clogged by hard-water deposits. Boil only the amount of water you need; it is a waste of heat to boil three pints of water for one cup of tea. Be sure, however, that you put in enough water to cover the element if your kettle is electric.

Oven savings

When you must use the oven to cook, for example, a roast joint or chicken, arrange to use the rest of the oven at the same time. You could cook vegetables to go with the meat, or you could bake flans or quiches for freezing to use later. Cakes, however, are not a good choice, as opening the oven door to baste the joint would not do the cake much good.

Saving with the fridge

Avoid allowing ice to build up into a thick layer – the thicker the ice the more electricity the fridge uses to freeze the food. Defrost regularly. Never put hot food into the fridge to cool; this has the same effect. Cool all food before refrigerating or freezing.

Improving the coal
Dissolve a handful of washing soda in half a bucket of warm water and pour it into your coal bunker. The burning power of the coal will be immensely improved by the time the soda-water has dried on the surface of the coal.

A cheap firelighter
A couple of moth-balls dropped on to a hot coal will revive a 'dead' fire at much less cost than using a firelighter. If the coal is not hot enough to ignite the moth-balls, drop a lighted match on them.

More coal-saving
Cut your coal bills by putting fire-bricks at the back of the grate. Much less coal is used in this way, and the bricks give out additional heat.

Instal a shower
A shower uses far less hot water than a bath – the only time the use of *running* hot water is justified!

Save with the TV
Switch on the TV only when you want to watch it. It is a complete waste of electricity leaving a TV on when no one is watching it. I never fail to be astonished by the mentality of people who leave it on all day, even when there is no one in the house, and then complain about their electricity bills.

Door curtains
The old-fashioned curtain of thick material hanging over a door did do quite a lot to keep the warmth inside the room. Why not consider this idea? It could save you quite a lot in heating bills.

Body insulation

Wear a cardigan, thicker skirts or trousers, thicker socks, stockings or tights, rather than turning up the central heating.

Immersion heaters

If you are lumbered with one of these horrendous electricity-bill boosters, at least remember to switch it off when the water is hot enough for your bath, clothes-washing or whatever. Use a kitchen timer.

Imitation fire-bricks

Save square or oblong cardboard packets from your groceries. Fill these with coal-dust and tiny pieces of coal, then dowse them thoroughly with the soda-water mixture described on page 000. Leave to dry, and use as fire-bricks. One in the middle of the fire will keep it going for about two hours without the addition of any more coal. Two at the back of the fire will put up the heat production by about 25%. Another good tip is to fill a paper bag with coal-dust and small pieces and put it in the middle of the fire, surrounded by larger pieces. When it burns right through, the glow will last for ages. Try it and see for yourself!

Another adaptation of the same idea is to punch a few holes in the bottom of any empty food-tin and fill that with dust and bits as before. Owing to the reflection of heat from the metal, the glow from this will last even longer.

Boiling is boiling!

Many people just do not realize that water boils at 100° C (212° F) and without pressure cannot become any hotter. Therefore it is just a waste of heat to keep gas or electricity burners going at full pelt after water, food or whatever has come to the boil. So long as bubbles are still to be seen escaping from the surface, the liquid is boiling. Adjusting the burner to such a level as to keep the liquid boiling will save heat. Keeping the heat very high will merely evaporate the liquid and thicken the mixture, and if continued to the point of evaporating *all* the liquid, you will just be left with a nice fat hole in the bottom of the pot. Some economy!

Don't buy a dishwashing machine
Even if you have a large family, this machine is an unnecessary waste of money both for the machine itself and the electricity needed to run it. The best dish-washer has two arms, two legs and wears a plastic apron, stacks the dishes at the side of the sink after rinsing and then dries them and puts them away in their proper places, which no machine can do. This model can be male or female, and is also far less likely to drop your best crockery or crack your best glasses. Training to become a model dishwasher can begin at the age of about four.

The airing cupboard
Line the walls of your airing cupboard with kitchen foil, pasted on the walls. They will reflect the heat from the hot pipes into the interior, thus increasing its drying power.

Poaching eggs en masse
If you have a large family but your egg-poacher contains only three or four depressions, you can poach eight eggs at a time in a very large soup saucepan and still use only one gas or electric ring. Grease the insides of eight ordinary tea or coffee cups and put the eggs in these. Stand them in the saucepan, pour water carefully in to cover the bottom to a depth of about an inch, bring to the boil and put on the lid. They may take slightly longer to cook, because china is a poor conductor of heat, unlike the metal egg-holders in the conventional egg-poacher.

Owing to the depth of china cups, you may find that there is too much egg white in proportion to the yolk when poaching eggs by this method. Pour some of the egg white into a basin, and by the time you have saved some from all the eggs you will have enough to make meringues!

Firelighters from milk cartons
Empty milk cartons, rinsed and flattened out, make excellent firelighters.

Saving at the stove
If you have a gas cooker, save spent matches for lighting an additional burner from the one you have in use.

Hot water bottles
Aluminium hot-water bottles retain heat far longer than rubber ones, although they are an awkward shape to cuddle! One can also be scalded more easily, so an aluminium bottle should wear a flannel cover.

Longer-lasting candles
Freeze candles before use and they will last much longer.

Anti-freeze for tanks and cisterns
Two teaspoons of glycerine to a lavatory cistern or outside tank will prevent them from freezing in winter. A drop or two in water-dishes provided for the birds (or your chickens) will also keep the water from freezing.

Pre-heating the oven
It is not necessary to preheat the oven except for fatless sponges, soufflés, and mixtures containing yeast.

Heavy cooking pans
Heavy-bottomed cooking pans save gas or electricity as they require less heat. The contents are also less prone to burning in a heavy pan.

Keep the lid on it!
Food will cook more quickly if you keep the lid on the pan. The heat can also be kept at a lower level to avoid food boiling over, as it is more apt to do in a lidded pan if the heat is too high. So by reducing the heat you also save on gas or electricity.

Two into one will go
By using a steamer you can boil one item in the lower pan and steam another item – a cauliflower, spinach, etc. – in the top part, at the same time. Try to choose two items which require approximately the same length of cooking time. Thus you cook two items for the cost of one in gas or electricity.

Fridge temperature
Don't run your fridge at a colder setting than necessary. The colder the setting, the more electricity it uses.

Upright or chest freezer?
Although an upright freezer takes up less floor space and is more convenient to use, a chest freezer costs less to buy and, what is more important, costs appreciably less to run.

Make full use of your freezer
It is uneconomical to run a freezer only half-full. You are paying for electricity to freeze empty air. Keep the freezer well-stocked.

Chapter Twelve

DIY

It is no exaggeration to say that vast savings can be made in the field of do-it-yourself painting and decorating, home-made furnishing and related areas. Just to give one example, a house owner who received an estimate running into four figures from a building firm (and a small building firm at that!) decided to do the job himself, with just the help of a student friend who had a better head for heights than he did and who would go up ladders for the upper floors. The job in question was completely repainting the exterior walls of the house, plus any re-pointing, re-fixing loose slates, etc. that might be necessary. He did the entire job for under two hundred pounds, which included the cost of all the materials, paying his student friend's 'wages' and the hire of a ladder. He thus saved himself more than eight hundred pounds, although he did admit that he took much longer than the builders might have done.

The same year I decided to re-paper one of the rooms in my abode. A college student acquaintance, who thought he was on to a good thing, offered to do the job for me for £100, and that was with the proviso that I should mix the paste and hold the other end of the strips of wallpaper for him! 'On your bike!' I said quickly, donning my apron, rolling up my sleeves and measuring up. 'I'll do the job myself for just the cost of the wallpaper and paste!' It took me five days, because the room is 30 ft long and 16 ft wide, and I suppose matching up the Regency stripes on the wallpaper made the job take rather longer than it would have done otherwise. Still, it just shows you what you can do if you put your mind to it.

On a smaller scale, you can save quite a lot of money in

other, less spectacular ways. First and foremost, *look after your tools*! It is no saving at all if you leave your tools out in the garden to rust, lose your nails and screws, and allow your cutting tools to become blunt and useless and have to replace all these things. Keep all tools under cover, and hang them up. A cold concrete floor in a garden shed is no place for them. A tool-box or chest will protect the small items, and larger ones such as saws should hang on the wall. Hang them on hooks, not nails, so that they do not slip off if knocked and injure somebody.

Keep nails, screws, bolts, nuts, hinges, etc. in separate containers – jam jars (with lids, to keep out the damp) are excellent as you can see what you have at a glance.

The business edges of saws should be lightly oiled when not in use. Vaseline, left-over fat from cooking, or any kind of oil will do. This keeps rust from attacking the cutting teeth.

Scissors and shears can be sharpened by drawing them back and forth over the neck of a bottle, as though trying to cut off the top of the bottle. Another method is to cut a piece of sandpaper several times, which soon gets a keen edge back on the blades.

Unless you are absolutely certain that your garden shed or workshop is absolutely insulated and damp-proof, do not keep power tools in it. Keep them indoors, along with any plugs, sockets, leads, transformers and extension coils.

S.O.S.
Save old screws! When dismantling secondhand wooden furniture, timber, etc., save all the old screws. If rusty, dip them in a paraffin bath and leave them overnight; this will remove the rust. These are small items but cost a lot these days and if you need many to do the job they may end up costing more than the wood!

Longer life for paintbrushes
Soak new paintbrushes in linseed oil overnight before use. This will make brushes last much longer.

First aid for brushes
If paintbrushes are stiff from disuse or clogged with
hardened paint, soak overnight in hot vinegar. They will
come out as good as new. Rinse with cold water before
using. The best thing is to avoid the brushes getting into
this sorry state in the first place. Don't just leave them to
go dry and hard, or stand them on end in a jar of water or
turps. The water or turps will evaporate and the brushes
will curl at the tips of the bristles where they touched the
bottom of the jar. Instead, wipe the brushes after use on
kitchen paper towel to remove most of the paint. Rinse
brushes used for emulsion painting in warm (not hot)
water, dry and hang up. Brushes which have been used for
gloss or other oil-based painting can be cleaned by subjec-
ting them to the vinegar treatment described at the
beginning of this paragraph.

Save on paint
When you have finished painting, press the lid on the can
firmly and reverse it, standing it upside-down on the
storage shelf. Any skin will thus form on the bottom
instead of the top. If only a small amount of paint is left,
decant this into a screw-top jar. If well-sealed a skin will
not form, and there will be less waste. It is a good idea to
keep such small jars of left-over paint for touching up any
scratches or marks after the painting job has been completed.

Avoid wasting paint while actually painting by tying a
string across the top of the paint tin so that you can wipe
the brush against this to stop drips.

Before you start painting, keep the tin of paint at room
temperature, unopened, for a few hours. This will make it
much easier to work with. If you are using an enamel
paint, stand the tin in a bowl of hot water. This will make
it go further, keep it thin enough to work with easily and
avoid the necessity of adding turps. It also enhances the
porcelain-like finish.

Don't use a roller and tray for painting small areas. This
wastes a lot of paint. It is only economical when used for

large areas. Line the tray with foil, then you will not have the tray full of multicolour dabs which may well dissolve in your next lot of turps and spoil the colour you are then using.

Save on plumbing

At least once a month throw a large handful of washing soda over the plug outlets of your kitchen sink, wash-basin and bath, and pour a full kettle of boiling water through each. This should keep your pipes clear of any blockage.

Learn to change a tap washer. This will save you paying a plumber to mend a dripping tap, which wastes water and, if it is a hot-water tap, gas or electricity. Some Water Boards fix dripping taps for free but not all. Ring your local Water Board to find out if they do the job free for anyone, or free for pensioners or the disabled. An appointment is necessary in any case. Some Water Boards do make a charge, but this is usually less than a private plumber would ask for the job.

Learn to change plugs and mend fuses

Ladies! Join the Electrical Association for Women. Join an evening class on home electrics. Changing plugs and mending fuses is not difficult BUT – you MUST remember to TURN OFF THE MAINS before you start, otherwise you might end up in smoke. The main thing (ouch!) is to remember the correct colours for live, earth and neutral.

Keeping putty

Putty will keep soft and pliable for up to a year if kept in kitchen foil, which must cover it completely to keep out air.

Hammering nails

Nails will go more easily into wood and avoid splitting the wood if they are pressed into a tablet of soap first.

A screw loose?
To loosen a screw which has rusted-in to the holes in the original wood, put the tip of a red-hot knitting-needle on the screw-head. The heat is transferred to the screw, which expands. When it cools it contracts, thus loosening it in the hole, so that it may be more easily removed.

Measure as you saw
Glue a tape-measure along the top edge of your saw. This is very useful. Use a good carpenter's tape, not a stretchy dressmaker's tape.

Damp-proofing a room before wallpapering
Coat the walls with sodium silicate (waterglass) before papering. Three coats are recommended. This will stop damp coming through the wallpaper. Allow each coat to dry out completely before applying the next one, and the paper.

Removing washable wallpapers
If removing washable papers before redecorating and they are difficult to remove, brush them with methylated spirits before soaking in the usual way, and they will come off much more easily. Only thing is, the place will stink like a shebeen for a day or two.

More wallpaper lore
If you have to patch wallpaper to hide a stain or rip, the edges will be far less conspicuous if you tear the edges of the patch in an regular manner rather than cutting a square or oblong piece. Be sure to match the pattern, too.

Store left-over rolls of wallpaper in old nylon stockings or nylon tights. These will keep the rolls clean when they are stored in a cupboard.

Staining floorboards
Before staining floorboards, apply an even coat of size, and allow it to harden for at least twenty-four hours. Then,

when you apply the stain, you will get a smoother finish, and the stain will go further, too.

Mending broken china
Make a paste with ground rice boiled in water until it thickens. China mended with this lasts years without further trouble.

Mending holes in saucepans
If the hole is only small, put a press-stud into it by putting one half of the stud on each side of the bottom of the pan and clipping them together. Then hammer flat on both sides. The pan will not leak.

Wall pictures from calendars
Many calendars have beautiful pictures – photographs, copies of Old Masters, etc. Frame them for wall pictures. Make your own frames, too, with a DIY framing-kit. These are so easy to do a child could make them.

A collage fire-screen
Paste a collage of glossy magazine pictures on an old fire-screen and give it a coat of varnish. Just the kind of thing teenagers might like to do. If the screen is to decorate your lounge, you may have to proscribe portraits of their favourite pop stars.

Cane chair seats
When these begin to sag, scrub the top and then the bottom with hot soapy water and dry the chair in the open air. This causes the cane to shrink and gives the chair a new lease of life.

Bedroom furniture face-lift
If you are fed up with your old bedroom furniture, paint it. Or you could strip it, stain it and varnish or French-polish it. It's cheaper than buying new furniture.

New place mats from old
If the pictures are peeling from your table mats, cover
them with brightly-coloured used postage stamps, and
give them a coat of clear varnish. These will make a
talking-point, too, if you use foreign stamps.

Old lampshades
Don't throw out your old lampshades. Take off the
covering material and staple muslin to the frames. These
now make good food-protectors to stop flies, wasps, etc.
getting at the food in the summer months. If preferred,
you can re-cover the frames with new material. Why not
make a new lamp-stand, too? An empty wine carafe or
other fancy-shaped bottle can be filled with brightly-
coloured glass beads, seaside pebbles and shells, or even
pasta shapes dyed with vegetable food colouring. This
makes a good, unusual stand.

Vinyl offcuts
The pieces left over from covering a floor with sheet vinyl
make good linings for cupboard shelves, easy to wipe
clean. Surplus vinyl tiles are even easier as they are self-
adhesive. Just cut to shape.

Spare ceramic tiles
If you have any of these to spare after tiling a wall, back
them with felt and they will make useful tea-pot or coffee-
pot stands.

Old tin cans
Used fruit cans in the larger sizes when painted make
plant-pot holders. The large-size coffee and biscuit tins
make good wastebaskets. These can be painted, or covered
with Fablon, material, strong paper such as vinyl wallpaper, or collages. Give the cans and the materials to the
children to keep them quiet! Make sure the cans have no
jagged edges.

Rawlplugs from pencil stubs
Save your old pencil stubs. Cut into various lengths, they make excellent rawlplugs. The graphite in the pencil lead helps to facilitate the entry of the nail, hook or screw, too.

Avoiding paint-drips on your step-ladder
Stand the paint-tin in one of those round foil dishes in which bakeries and supermarkets sell flans and pies. If you bake all your own pies and flans, just make a little dish of foil a little larger all round than the paint tin.

Maritime protection
If your house is on the sea front or any other position exposed to salt breezes, cover all external paintwork with a coat of boat varnish. It will last up to three times as long without the need for re-painting. Inland, a good wash with soapy water will brighten up external paintwork to the extent that you may well find it unnecessary to renew the paintwork for another year.

Not lost but found
When decorating or doing other DIY work, keep a small box at hand. Into this go all the odd bits and pieces, finger-plates, switch-plates, nails, screws, hooks, handles, etc. which you have to remove in order to paint or repair the wall, door or whatever.

A temporary seal for paint tins
Cover tightly with foil until you are ready to continue painting.

Drilling holes in plaster
To stop plaster cracking and chipping when drilling a hole in the wall, stick a small piece of Sellotape over the place where you want the hole to be before you start the drilling operation.

Window-ledges

Painted ledges peel and chip. It's almost impossible to prevent this. It's because of their immediate proximity to air and moisture and exposure to extremes of temperature. Tile them, and they will always look good – easier to keep clean, too.

Wallpaper leftovers

Before giving the remainder of the roll to the children to play with, be sure to keep some in case you need to patch a damaged or stained part later. If this occurs very much later, the new paper patch may be brighter than the slightly-faded paper on the wall. 'Fade' the new patch to match the original by painting it with lemon juice.

Protecting the carpet when painting

Stick masking tape or wide Sellotape on the edge of the carpet before attempting to paint the skirting-boards. When decorating the ceiling cover the entire carpet with black plastic rubbish-bags, *not* white sheets or other cloth material. Emulsion paint goes right through cloth, but plastic will give complete carpet protection.

Painting windows

When painting window-frames stick masking tape or wide Sellotape on the glass around the edges of each pane to avoid getting paint on the glass.

Emulsion painting

If you cannot complete the job all in one go, wrap the brush tightly in foil to prevent the emulsion paint hardening the bristles until you are ready to recommence painting.

Gloss painting

Brushes used for gloss or oil-based paints need different treatment. Suspend the brush in a jar of water or paraffin. Do not let the bristles touch the bottom of the jar. It is a good idea to buy brushes with holes in the tops of the handles as this makes for easy suspension. They can also be hung up after use, cleaned and dried, on a nail or hook kept for the purpose.

Measurements

Keep a log book containing the measurements of all your rooms, the number of rolls of wallpaper needed for each, the number of pints or gallons of paint needed. This will save you a lot of bother (and arithmetic) next time you wish to redecorate your house or flat.

Barter your skills

If your neighbour, friend or relative is a dab hand with the paintbrush but you can't manage the job without slopping paint all over the floor (like me), and you are good at wallpapering single-handed (also like me) but he can't put up wallpaper for toffee, you do his or her wallpapering in return for the painting job. You can also barter the loan of tools. Maybe your friend has a power drill or a chainsaw but no lawn-mower or hedge-cutters (which you have) and so you can agree to swap on a temporary basis. This saves paying people to do the jobs you cannot do or buying tools you may need to use only once, on both sides.

Pictures for the walls

If you go to enough jumble sales you will eventually find one which has old engravings and hand-coloured plates, old Victorian and Edwardian photographs and etchings, etc. for sale at bargain prices. These, framed, make marvellous wall pictures, especially if you are a lover of antiques anyway.

Old frames may also be found at jumble sales and in junk shops. Market stalls selling secondhand goods also frequently have some. If you do not like the picture it can easily be removed and something else substituted more to your taste.

Roller blinds
Make your own from craft-shop kits. These will work out
vastly cheaper than buying ready-made ones.

Salvaging old wood
Before chopping up old chairs and burning them on the
fire or in the boiler, look first to see whether any of the
parts would provide pieces of wood for other purposes.
This does not apply only to chairs, of course. Shelves, for
example, could be made from the bottoms of old drawers
from a tallboy that you no longer need.

A bookcase in ten minutes
You need clean planks about 9 in wide, of various lengths;
some new bricks (or old ones covered with wallpaper,
brown parcel-wrapping paper, Christmas giftwrap paper
(save this from your presents), Fablon, (or even double-
thickness foil); and ten minutes of your valuable time to
arrange them in any convenient way, such as, for example,
the design shown at Fig.8. Stand the whole thing firmly
against a wall so that it does not fall over, and do not be
tempted to make the brick stacks too high, as this will
reduce stability. The advantage of not joining everything
permanently together is that you can move it into a
different arrangement, a different position in the room, or
even a different room, as and when desired. Stain and
polish the shelves for maximum effect, and use heavy
plant pots (with trailing plants) as book-ends. A long, low
arrangement is the safest to use, and always have bricks at
the ends for support.

Fig. 8

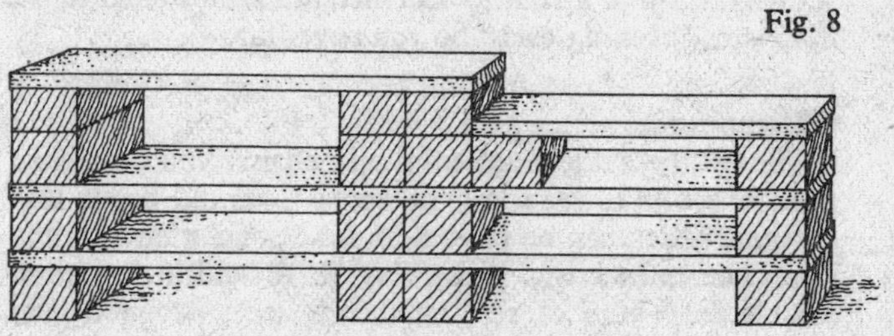

Repairing a deck chair

Before attaching the new material, fasten a strip of felt or foam rubber around the top and bottom bars. This will save wear and tear on the new material. Buy double the length of striped deck-chair canvas you would normally buy, and fold it so that you have a double thickness of material, with the covered bars inside, on the same principle as a roller towel. You will find that the material lasts more than twice as long, and the padded bars will also make the deck chair more comfortable in use.

Painting or staining a floor

It's amazing how many do-it-yourselfers, especially raw beginners, start painting or staining a floor at the door end. If you do this, you'll need a helicopter to get you out when you get to the far end.

Old sofas and easy chairs

I'm amazed at how many old sofas and easy chairs I see on the council rubbish-dump which are perfectly sound except for the webbing or the cover. Upholstery is, admittedly, not as easy as it looks, but it can be learned, either from a book or, better still, from an evening class where you will at least have some old crocks to practise on until you dare attempt your own. Have a go! If you can find someone to transport the castaway from the rubbish-tip to your home, you can have a new sofa or chairs (or both) for free, except for what you spend to buy new webbing or covering material and upholstery tacks. I actually know a girl who met her future husband at an upholstery evening class! So you never know . . .

Chairback and settee sets

While on the subjects of sofas and chairs, you can make attractive sets to hang on the backs from old heavy lace curtains which can be picked up for a song at any jumble sale. The ones I was lucky enough to find at a church jumble sale were of real handmade lace, probably late nineteenth century. On the same occasion I picked up a sixteen-piece coffee-set for a pound.

Looking after leather chairs
These, which get a lot of use, especially if placed near a fireside, are apt to crack and look unsightly. Prevent this by rubbing them with a clean cloth dipped in glycerine from time to time. Following this treatment, leave for a few hours, or overnight, then polish with a soft dry cloth.

DIY books
Every public library I have ever used has a large and comprehensive section of DIY books, both general and on specific subjects such as carpentry and woodwork, crafts, furniture repairs, etc. Save money by resisting the temptation to buy the lavishly-illustrated books available on the subject from your booksellers, and borrowing them free from the library. But remember to renew them regularly: you don't want to nullify your saving by paying library fines!

Rips in leather and vinyl chairs
These can be repaired by cutting a strip of two-inch wide self-adhesive binding tape under the tear, pressing the raw edges over it so that no gap shows. Hold the pressure until the torn edges do not slip. Keep the kids from climbing all over the chairs and sofas in the first place and do not let them run toy cars and other things which may have sharp edges over them.

Scratched wood furniture
A mixture of olive oil and vinegar rubbed well into the wood often removes light scratches. For deeper and more conspicuous scratches, try rubbing in shoe polish of the same shade as the wood, and then polish over in both cases.

Scratches and chips on enamel
To cover scratches or chips on white enamel fridges, cookers, etc., paint with opaque white nail varnish. My

secondhand fridge-freezer, which was scratched to death when I bought it (that's why I got it for one-eighth of the new price), now looks like a new one after the nail-varnish treatment.

Cutting down to size

Those huge, old-fashioned, cumbersome Victorian wardrobes go for a song these days. Nobody wants a gigantic thing like that taking up valuable space. Buy it anyway and you can cut off the bottom to make a storage chest and the top to make an attractively-carved hanging shelf. The body will make a window-seat, an ottoman and a single wardrobe! You will also be able to salvage an assortment of hinges and screws, and probably antique or semi-antique door-handles, locks and keys.

I once bought a house and found that the vendor had left one of these monstrosities in the main bedroom, thinking that he was well rid of it without the hassle of getting it down the stairs, which would have been a physical impossibility anyway. I cut it into these various items as mentioned above, and the vendor and his wife, who came to see me after I had settled in and converted the house into a small private school for ESN children, never recognized any of the five new items!! I might add that no painting or staining was necessary – the wardrobe had been made of solid mahogany throughout. It polished up beautifully with furniture cream.

From office to home

Look in secondhand office furniture dealers' shops. Wooden filing cabinets, painted, make super children's room chests of drawers. The smaller two-drawer kinds make a desk for a child's room. You need two of them, plus a board to lay across the top. Paint the whole thing. If the child is young, it is better to screw the drawer units to the top to avoid the child pulling the top off. An artistic teenager might like to have a draughtsman's blueprint chest to keep his or her drawings and paintings in laid flat. The cabinet can be painted to match the rest of the decor.

Typists' swivel chairs are good in teenage students' rooms, but they should be of good strong construction, preferably stainless steel with vinyl padded seat and back, and adjustable seat-height and backrest-angle mechanism.

The hat-and-coat stands sold for office use make splendid plant-stands for the home. The hooks are at just the right heights for hanging plant baskets! Sometimes these stands are of mahogany, redwood or other good wood and need only polishing; others, of the more common-or- garden kind, may look tatty unless given a coat of paint to tone with your colour scheme, or are stripped, sanded and varnished with matt varnish (which allows the original grain of the wood to show through without its being obscured by a high gloss).

Makeshift tables and chairs

If you're just starting out to build a home of your own, or have to furnish a temporary abode cheaply pending some better permanent arrangement, a makeshift table can be made by laying a flush door on top of a tea-chest and screwing it into position. Then cover the whole thing with a floor-length table-cloth! No one, but no one is going to go down on hands and knees to peer under the table. Just make sure they don't drop anything. A round piece of wood or even thick chipboard, stood on top of a long wooden box up-ended, the whole covered with a floor-length round tablecloth, makes a very good corner table. Stand a plant on top. For a coffee-table, cut off the legs of an ordinary table to the desired height. Any old scratched table will do – you hide all the blemishes by covering the entire top with those tiny mosaic tiles. If the legs are a bit grotty, paint them first with an enamel paint in a blending shade.

Why worry that the chairs are all different shapes? Just co-ordinate them into a harmonious whole by painting them all the same colour.

A makeshift clothes unit

This needs no description. Just lash twelve broom-handles

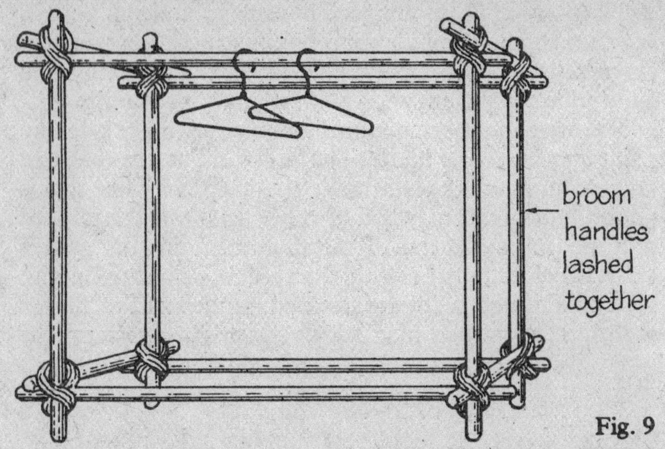

Fig. 9

together as shown in Fig. 9. A double half-hitch is best (I hope you know your knots!) A good strong cord should be used. You could paint the broom-handles before you make the unit, and use gold cord to lash them together. Teenagers could put one of these together in less time than it takes to say 'Knots landing!'

If there is an alcove or recess in the room, just fix a dowel rod between the two walls at wardrobe-rail height in the alcove. Then just screw two hooks into the wall, one at each end, on the side facing the rest of the room, and stretch a wire curtain-hanger (called in some places 'expanding wire rod') between the two hooks to support a sliding curtain to cover the alcove and keep out at least some of the dust. A shelf could be fitted at the bottom, about a foot or so from the floor, for shoes, handbags, etc. A few suction hooks on the rear wall of the recess will be useful for hanging various things out of the way.

A new use for garden trellis
This is very useful screwed to the wall, especially in the kitchen, with hooks screwed into it at various intervals to hang cups, mugs, soup ladles, slotted spoons, etc. Bills can be pushed behind the wooden partitions, where they

will remain visible and thus ensure that you pay them, not mislay them!

Shelving on the cheap

Timber offcuts are the basis for your shelving. Buy them at bargain prices, sand, stain and varnish them or paint them. You may be lucky enough to find offcuts in attractive knotty pine, as I was able to do. These need only sealing with transparent matt sealing-varnish. Then you put up brackets to take them. The really enterprising will be able to find brackets, screws and other metal accessories on a building or demolition site, and de-rust them in paraffin if necessary. If secondhand brackets look a bit grotty, paint them. Brass ones may be polished with Brasso and chromium ones come up very well rubbed with a paste made of soda and water (baking, not washing, soda).

If you are fortunate enough to obtain really long offcuts of timber, remember that a long shelf should really have an additional bracket supporting it in the middle, or it will sag under any constant heavy weight such as books. If only comparatively light articles are going to be placed on it, such as glass ornaments, etc., you could probably do without a middle bracket.

Darkening stained floors

If you wish to darken a newly-sanded floor and bring out the grain of the original wood, rub with neat linseed oil. When the floor has dried polish with a beeswax polish.

Save those tiles!

If you have to drill a hole in anything with a slippery surface such as ceramic tiles, put a strip of insulation tape over the area to be drilled. This will prevent the tile from cracking or splitting. Afterwards the tape can be peeled off easily.

Holes in wood

Fill with putty rather than powdered filler. Then, when you paint over the filled-in hole with gloss paint, the surface remains glossy instead of the paint being absorbed into the filling material.

Stripping the bed
I here refer to a brass bedstead! You may be lucky enough to find one going comparatively cheaply secondhand because it has at one time been lacquered. By removing the lacquer, you will have – would you believe it? – a gleaming brass bedstead! But – and this is a big but – do *not* use paint-stripper, or you will ruin the brass. Rub with surgical spirit. It *will* come off eventually, but the operation is rather time-consuming. This is a good task for a team!

So far, bargain brass bedsteads have happened to everyone except me. I'm still looking!

A sanding tip
Always sand *with* the grain of the wood, otherwise you will scratch it. Fasten the sandpaper round a block of wood for easy handling, to give an even surface.

. . . and one for the saw
Keep the stump of an old candle in your toolbox and before using the saw rub the candle along each side of the blade a few times. This will make the operation of sawing considerably easier. Do not use on a chainsaw.

Conveyor-belt style . . .
When putting up shelves, complete each process all through before starting another one: thus, do all the sawing at one go, then all the drilling, and so on. This is much less time-consuming than continually changing the drill bits, reaching for different tools, putting them down and taking them up again, and so on. It is also less fatiguing as you will not have to be constantly changing position. The safest way is to put the tools away as soon as you have finished with them, and unplug and return all power tools to their places.

Rawlplug substitutes

Pencil-stubs, spent matches, pieces of hollow plastic washing-line, pieces of plastic tubing, pieces of twigs – all cut to suitable sizes. I find that wooden plugs are much better, firmer and easier to work with than plastic ones, but I know a carpenter who swears the opposite!

Wallpaper paste

When you have finished papering, put any leftover paste into a screwtop jar in case you have to 'touch up' any piece that becomes unstuck, a corner that comes loose, or minor repairs. If you leave it in an open container it will dry up.

A storage shelf for the workshop

To the underside of an eye-level shelf in your workshop screw the lids of glass jars. The jars themselves then screw into the lids on the underside of the shelf, and can similarly be unscrewed when the contents are required. Into these jars you put nails, screws, panel pins, carpet tacks, brads, etc., all sorted into sizes and labelled with the size. You can also see at a glance when you are running out of stock of any particular item.

The same idea can be used in the kitchen to contain spices, or, with larger jars, pulses. Dried herbs can be similarly stored.

At the end of the shelf attach a much larger jar. This contains a ball of string. Drill a hole through the shelf and through the middle of the lid of the jar. The end of the string protrudes through from the jar to the upper surface of the shelf, and the string can never become tangled. All you have to do is pull and cut off the exact length required.

Drawers that stick

Rub a candle along the *bottom* edges of the drawer. Soap will do if you haven't a candle. But you should in any case always keep a few candles, in case of a power cut.

Cutting polystyrene tiles
When you have to cut these to fit, dip the knife in boiling water. This will prevent the tiles from cracking or splitting.

Removing dried emulsion paint
If you slop this on your clothes, the floor, carpets, etc. while painting (join the club!) it will come off with methylated spirits, even when completely dried. Getting it on your hair would be more tricky, and I don't honestly think that meths would make a very good shampoo! The best thing to do is to wear a plastic bag on your head while painting!

A tip for the home plumber
Having released the screw from the U-bend of a waste pipe, grease the thread with vaseline before re-screwing into place. This will make it easier to unscrew next time, if there is one.

Rehanging pictures after papering
If you want to rehang a mirror, pictures, etc. on the wall in the same position after repapering as they were before, insert a cocktail stick into the hole where the picture-hook was nailed before you stripped the wall. The stick will then protrude through the new wallpaper and enable you to see at a glance where to rehang the picture. Make a pencil dot in the position, withdraw the cocktail stick, and smooth the wallpaper on the wall.

A heavy mirror, or a large picture in a heavy antique frame, will often mark the wallpaper. This can be avoided by gluing narrow strips of foam rubber along the edges of the back of the frame.

Space-saving in cupboards
A lot of space can be saved by screwing hooks on the insides of cupboard doors. In the kitchen these will take whisks, beaters, kitchen knives, your cooking thermometer, spare dishtowels, etc. In the wardrobe they will

take scarves, ties, hats, shoulder-bags, belts, and so on. If you have a broom cupboard, glue or screw two cotton-reels (empty) together in such a way that there is just enough space between them to take a broom handle. The broomhead then sits on top of the cotton-reels with the handle between them. Mops, etc. can also be suspended in the same way. This then leaves more space for such items as the Hoover, buckets, and so on.

Light objects can be suspended from suction-pad hooks which are simply stuck to the inside of the door. These can take overalls, aprons, laundry-bags and carrier bags containing your cleaning cloths, dusters, etc.

It pays to be ingenious and find such simple ways of getting more storage space into every available spot. In my family, we have coined the word 'splodge', which means anything that is not in its proper place (usually out of sight). Wage war on splodge, and you will have a neat and uncluttered home. That oft-quoted 'lived-in look' does *not* mean your sewing strewn about the room, Johnny's Lego all over the floor and Jane's tights swinging from the shower-rail!

Chapter Thirteen

The Garden

The garden is one of the areas in which the most savings can be effected by recycling existing materials.

Getting down to basics, gardening starts with the soil. There is absolutely no need at all to buy commercial compost – you can make your own from recycled kitchen wastes. Once you have all the ingredients of good compost, you can even make your own soil!

The compost bin

Before making your own compost, first of all build a compost bin, using odds and ends of chicken wire and four stakes. Drive these into the ground to form a square having sides not less than 2ft long, and staple the wire netting to them, thus forming a well-ventilated enclosure (Fig. 10). Four feet is a convenient height. If you make it any higher you will find if difficult to get a garden fork into it to turn the compost, or a spade into it when it is ready for digging into the garden. The netting sides not only allow proper ventilation but also stop the material you dump into the bin from blowing about in the wind and making the garden untidy, as well as encouraging pests such as slugs which are attracted to rubbish lying about on top of the soil.

Compost

Anything organic should be thrown into the bin – tea leaves, coffee grounds, outside cabbage leaves which are too coarse to cook, hedge clippings, lawn mowings and other grass cuttings, weeds, dust from your vacuum cleaner, fallen leaves, old used soil full of dead roots from defunct pot plants, even newspaper (which is derived from wood). Newspaper decomposes more slowly than some

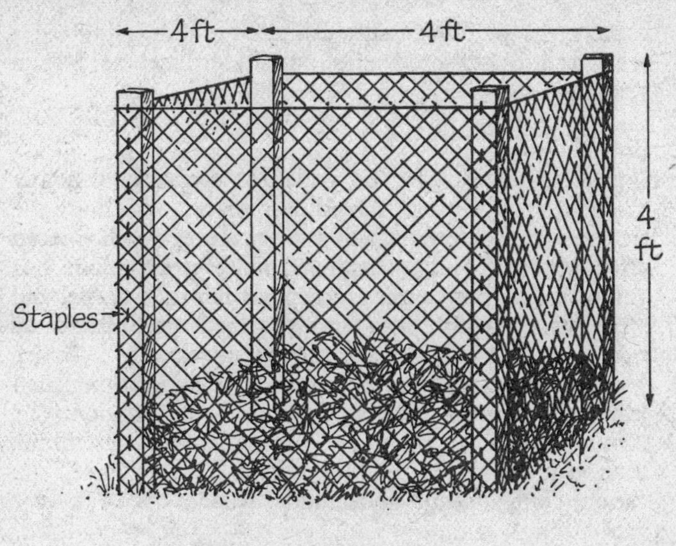

Compost bin from 4 stakes
and 16 ft. of chicken-wire

Fig. 10

other materials and to hasten this process it should be torn into small pieces. However, since newspaper has a great many other uses (see Chapter Nine), first see if there are any better ways in which you can re-use it before finally deciding to add it to the compost heap.

The compost should be turned with a fork from time to time in order to assist its decomposition by aerobic bacteria. As soon as it has thoroughly rotted it forms a sweet-smelling dark soil rich in humus and nutrients, and can then be dug into the garden to improve the soil, or used as soil where there is none. The process takes anything from nine to twelve months depending on the materials used and the weather conditions.

Eggshells are a good source of lime, and if you do not want to use them to make the lime fertilizer described later in this chapter under *Fertilizers*, the eggshells should first be crushed as small as possible before being added to the compost heap. Wood ashes can also be added, but these are much better used as a potash fertilizer as I shall describe later.

Soil

A good soil mixture can be made by blending your home-made compost with crumbled dead leaves, which are the richest source of humus, and horse manure, which you can often obtain free from riding stables if you collect it yourself. Another source is to collect it with a trowel and some strong plastic bags in woodlands frequented by riders and on moorlands used by pony-trekkers.

Most park gardeners will let you have some of the fallen leaves they sweep up every autumn if you provide your own plastic bags, but if you are diffident about asking them you can always collect dead leaves yourself on various commons and in deciduous woods.

Fertilizers

Purchasing commercial fertilizers is totally unnecessary. If your soil is rich in compost, humus and manure you should not need any, except perhaps for lime and potash. Crush eggshells as finely as possible and use in the same way as you would use lime; the effect is the same. Wood ash left after burning logs in your fireplace, in a wood-burning boiler or on a bonfire, is a potash-rich fertilizer which can be spread around the roots of vegetables. Charcoal pieces found among the wood ashes are excellent for sweetening the soil in houseplant pots.

Another home-made fertilizer can be made from lawn mowings or other grass cuttings. Leave them to decompose in an old bucket of water for a couple of weeks or so until fermented. This should be done well away from the house, as the solution stinks! However, it makes a very fine green liquid manure, and after it has been applied to the soil the stench soon disappears.

Stinging-nettles can be used in the same way. They take longer to decompose – up to three weeks – and the smell is no better. The green sludge-like mixture is used as a mulch, being spread on the surface of the soil around the plants. If strained the liquid can be used as an anti-blackfly spray for broad beans, if you can bring yourself to put up with the nauseating odour while you are doing the spraying. If not, ordinary soapsuds will put paid to blackfly but may require more than one application. Note that *soap* must be used, not detergent powders.

If you live near the sea, you have a vast supply of superb fertilizer free for the gathering. Seaweed is even richer than farmyard manure. It should be dug straight into the soil as soon as it has been gathered. Do not leave it around to be dug in later as the nutrients soon dry out.

Tea leaves, mentioned already as a compost ingredient, can also be used alone as a specific pick-me-up for rose bushes. The quickest and easiest way is to empty the teapot around the roots of the bushes, after the gardener has first enjoyed his own pick-me-up!

When planting peas or beans in trenches, torn pieces of newspaper may be laid along the bottoms of the trenches, the soil piled back in on top and the peas or beans then planted. Nutrients from the wood-derived newspaper will slowly leach out into the soil over a long period. This is more of a long-term fertilizing plan than a rapid-acting one.

Watering

From soil and fertilizers to watering. Rainwater is much better than tap water for plants and should be saved in a water-butt, placed strategically beneath a pipe leading from the roof gutter. To stop gnats laying their eggs and breeding in the water-butt, cover it with fine rustproof copper wire mesh (or aluminium mesh), or with a thin film of oil on the surface of the water which will effectively prevent gnat larvae from breathing.

If you have an old garden hose which is worn out and no longer able to do its job, make a few more holes in it in addition to the ones it has already, at intervals along the length of the hose from the point at which you need to water the garden. Obviously you should not start making these too near the end you attach to the water tap, or you will have fountains where they are not particularly ornamental, and a shower in the kitchen. By recycling the old hose into a lawn or flowerbed sprinkler, you are now enabled to leave it unattended to water the garden while you attend to some other job. All you need to do is to turn the tap on or off as the case may be.

Automatic watering device

Now what about rigging up an automatic plant-waterer for your houseplants, pot tomatoes, etc. while you are away on holiday? You do not need to waste money on costly commercial gadgets sold for the purpose. All you need is a large jug of water and as many lengths of string as you have pots to be watered. The jug should be full, and should be stood on a ledge or shelf higher than the pots to be watered. One end of each piece of string should be placed in the jug, making sure that the end touches the bottom. The other end should lie on the surface of the soil in the pot. The string will act as a wick, water being slowly absorbed into the soil. The reason for ensuring that the end of the string in the water reaches the bottom of the jug is, of course, to avoid its being left high and dry as the water evaporates. You need never again come home from your holiday to stand aghast at the sight of all your dead plants!

Tools

A good many tools essential to the gardener can be recycled from various odds and ends, thus saving considerable sums of money.

Soil sifter

A metal mesh kitchen strainer which has rusted and so can no longer be used for its original purpose can be used in the garden for sifting fine soil on to seed boxes when seeds require only a very light dusting of soil.

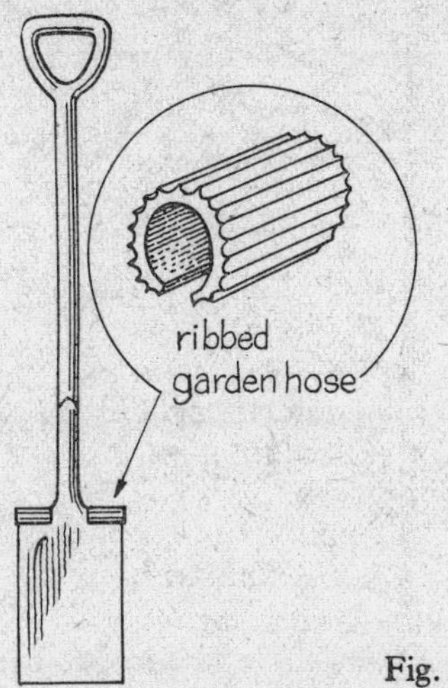

Fig. 11

Footwear protection when digging

A good way of saving wear and tear on boots and shoes when digging is to split a piece of old unwanted garden hose along one side and fit this along the upper edge of the blade of the spade, cutting one piece to fit on each side of the handle joint (Fig. 11). This saves a great deal of friction on the sole of the boot or shoe at the point where the foot is placed for making the spade thrusts when digging.

Foot-operated dibber

The tedious chore of dibbing holes for the planting of large seeds such as peas and beans or for transplanting them from small pots into their permanent positions can be greatly reduced by recycling an old broom handle and a small shelf bracket into a foot-operated dibber. Whittle the broom handle to a point at one end, and screw a small metal shelf bracket about 9 in above the point to form a footrest (Fig. 12). It is also a useful idea to mark off the broom handle in inches or centimetres (whichever you

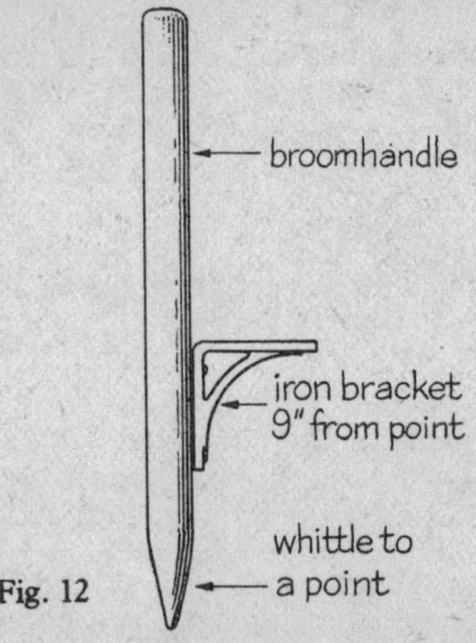

use) as a guide to planting depth and for plotting distances between the holes or between the drills or rows.

Garden markers
These are easily made from children's lollipop sticks, which require no cutting, or from plastic yoghourt, cottage cheese or margarine tubs from which they can be easily cut out with ordinary kitchen scissors. Use an indelible pencil to write on plastic.

Transplanter for small seedlings
An old carving fork no longer needed in the kitchen or dining-room makes a splendid tool for transplanting small and delicate seedlings from their first position in seedbox, yoghourt tub or small pot to their final position. The long narrow prongs of the carving fork make it easy to lift the plantlet by sliding them along the surface of the soil on each side of the seedlings. Each seedling can then be separately lifted at this delicate stage without injury to the roots or snapping the frail stems.

Garden ties

Discarded tights and nylons can be cut into narrow strips to use as garden ties. Nylon is so strong that the ties are unlikely ever to break. (In a gardening book I read once the author said we should use 'discarded ladies' tights'!)

Mini-hoe for seedboxes

Heat the blade of an old knife in a flame and bend over the top two inches to an angle of 45 degrees. You now have a natty little mini-hoe!

Trug for garden use

A garden trug may be made from a wooden seedbox by adding a handle from scrap wood (Fig. 13).

Water spray for the greenhouse

An empty squeezy bottle such as the kind which once contained washing-up liquid makes an ideal greenhouse spray.

Fruit picking stick with collecting bag

Fig. 14 shows how to make a useful fruit picker with attached bag which (hopefully) catches the fruit when picked instead of allowing it to drop to the ground and become bruised. The stick should be as long as you can conveniently handle. In practice it should not be *too* long, as it then becomes unwieldy to use. I think about 8ft is

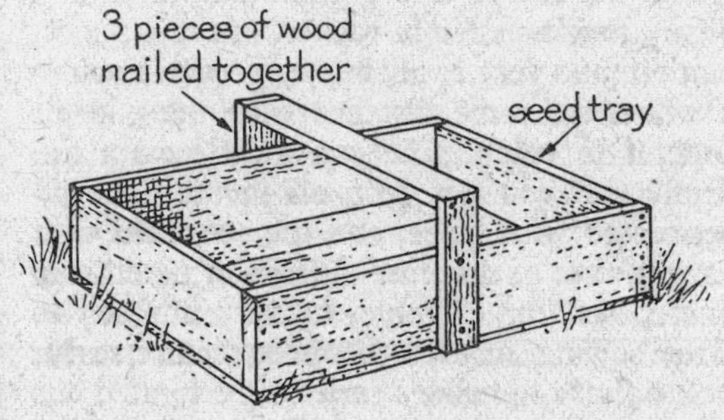

Fig. 13

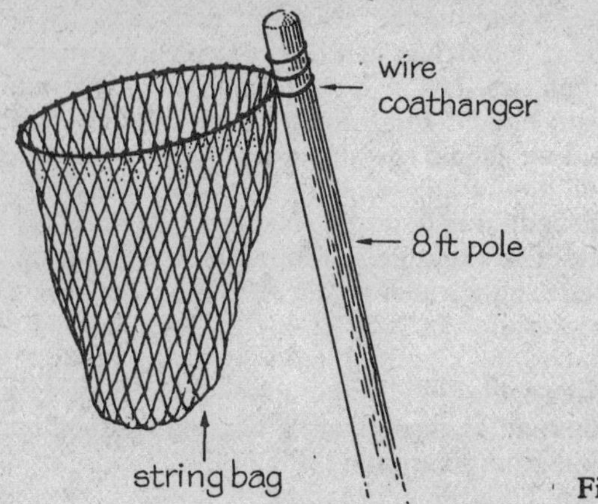

long enough – if you need to reach fruits higher on the tree you need a stepladder.

Bend a wire coathanger into a circle and twist the hook part round one end of the stick about 4 in from the end. Attach a string shopping bag (preferably of nylon for strength) around the wire circle with a staple gun. You then gently knock the stem of the apple, pear, etc. with the end of the stick and pray that it drops straight into the bag. It usually does.

Garden dispenser
A tin can tied to the end of a long stick (Fig. 15) looks rather like a Guy Fawkes's Night rocket, but it is a most useful contraption (and very easily made) to enable you to reach plants which are some distance from the path or otherwise difficult to reach. The can must have a lid, which fits firmly and will not drop off in use. The lid should be perforated with holes, and the can filled with whatever it is you want to dispense – derris or pyrethrum powder against pests, for example, or very fine soil to cover seeds after sowing, or even the seeds themselves! It is therefore a good idea to make a series of perforated lids

with the holes of varying sizes according to the material to
be dispensed.

Hanging potholders
These can be fashioned from wire coathangers by twisting
them into a circle to hold the plant pot and the remainder
into whatever shape you require to fit the space concerned.
Any excess can be cut off with tinsnips. The two ends can
be formed into eyelets to enable the potholder to be
hooked on to nails in the wall. The ingenious can make
one coathanger into a double potholder to support two
small pots, either one above the other or horizontally, by
twisting it into two circles. You can paint the potholders
white or green if you want to.

Row markers and training wire pegs
Old metal meat skewers can be used for stretching string
or garden twine along rows to mark out the position of
drills of seeds. They will not rust, snap or bend so are
much better than sticks, and are also less likely to be
pulled out of the soil by wind or washed out in a storm.
Another use for metal skewers is to stretch training wires
along a wall for cordon and espalier fruit trees. To make
them into wall pegs just snip them to the length required
with wirecutters and drive them into the mortar with a
hammer or heavy mallet.

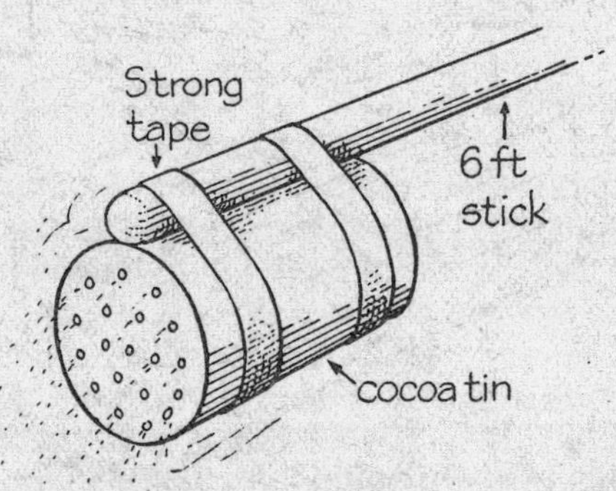

Fig. 15

Window boxes

Make your own window boxes from old floorboards by nailing them together, then screwing the corners together for added strength, as a window box full of soil can be very heavy, especially after watering. You don't want the thing to crash to the ground from your high-level flat on to some unsuspecting person's head. Don't forget to drill holes in the bottom of the window box for drainage. If water falls on the passer-by's head it at least will not kill him, even if it spoils his new hat. If you have no drill the holes can be burned through with a red-hot poker. Paint the window box inside with a non-toxic wood preservative (which you can make from equal parts of paraffin and used car engine sump oil) and the outside with any lead-free paint to blend with the external décor of the house or flat.

Cold frames

These are simplicity itself to rig up from old bricks and window frames. Simply lay two courses of bricks, but without using any mortar, so that you can dismantle the whole thing when you no longer need it or you want to move it to a different part of the garden. The window frame is then just laid on the top (Fig. 16). For ventilation

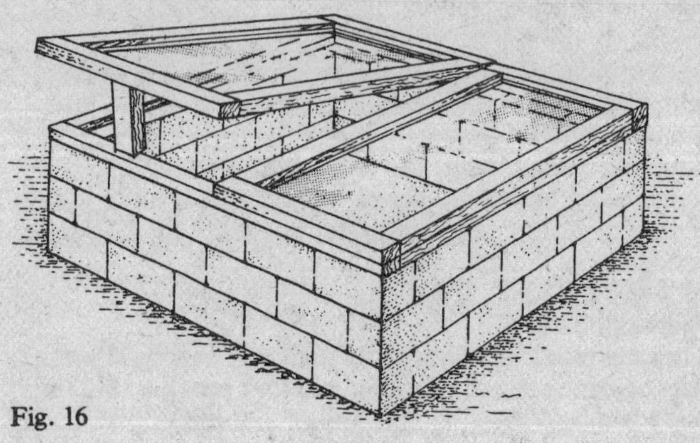

Fig. 16

when required you just prop it up with a piece of wood, as shown in the same figure.

Plant pots

The things you can recycle for use as plant pots are legion.

For large sizes, the plastic buckets in which various building compounds and adhesives are sold are ideal for growing tomatoes, mushrooms, etc. in the greenhouse. Punch holes in the bottom for drainage. Smaller pots can be made from tin cans, yoghourt tubs, cheese boxes, cottage cheese and margarine tubs, and the bottoms of plastic squeezy bottles (just cut off the top, leaving a deep enough portion to form the pot). Punch holes in the bottoms of all these containers. In the case of tin cans, cut the lids out cleanly without leaving any jagged edges. The various supermarket trays and dishes made of plastic and styrofoam also make useful containers for small seedlings.

Do not use very deep tubs, or cut plastic bottles too high up so that the part you are going to use as a plant pot is too deep, as this will block out light from the growing seedling.

If your containers are to be stood on the window-ledge in the house or flat you can decorate them if you wish by sticking on pieces of self-stick Fablon, or by painting them to match the décor.

Egg-boxes made from papier mâché can be used like peat pots. Sow seeds in compost, one in each of the six sections, and when the plants are ready to be transplanted cut the egg-boxes into their six separate sections and plant straight into the garden as you would a peat pot. The papier mâché is biodegradable and as it rots it will gradually release nutrients derived from the wood which was the primary source material for its manufacture. These nutrients will fertilize your soil. The styrofoam or plastic egg-boxes are unsuitable for this purpose, of course.

Propagator-tops

The clear plastic prop-tops sold to fit over various standard sizes of plant pots are very good and look very nice but they cost a bomb. With wire, plastic bags and rubber bands you can make your own. The wire can be salvaged from unwanted wire clotheshangers. Snip into suitable lengths and bend into two hoops as shown in the diagram (Fig. 17) which shows the completed prop-top made by putting a plastic bag over the hoops and securing it round the rim of the pot with a strong elastic band. I say 'strong' because a flimsy one will soon rot from the damp.

Cloches

A wire coathanger (these do seem to be jolly useful around the garden!) and two pieces of unwanted picture framing glass can be recycled into a cloche. The method is clearly

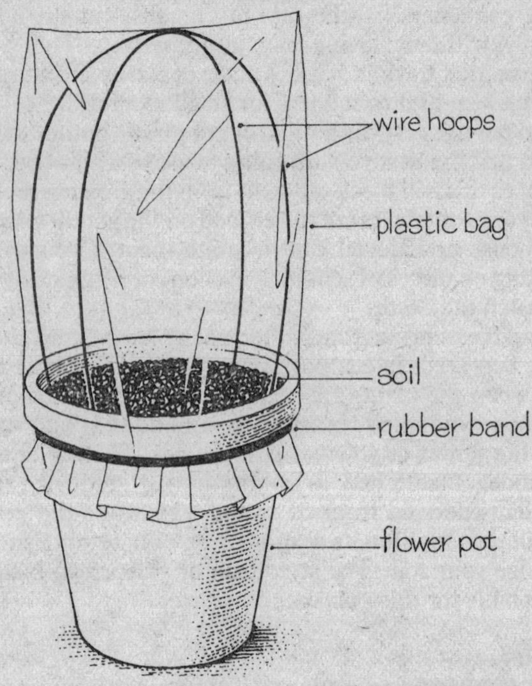

Fig. 17   Making your own plant propagator from re-cycled materials

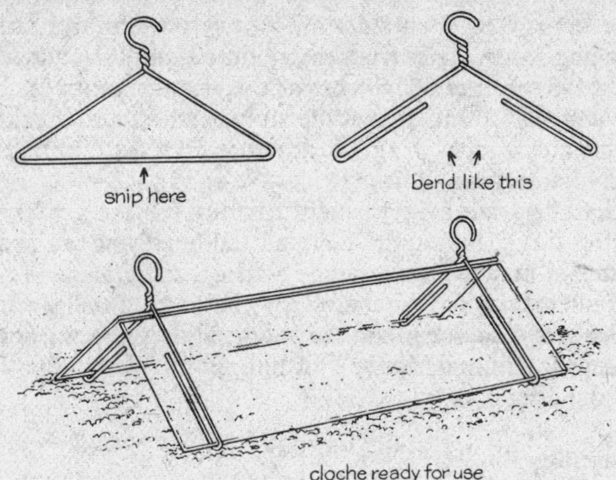

Fig. 18

shown in the diagram at Fig. 18 and needs no further description. Old framed pictures with glass are frequently to be picked up for pennies on secondhand stalls in markets, in junk shops and at bric-à-brac auction sales. The wire coathangers are usually given away free by dry cleaners. I have often seen quantities of them in dustbins outside dry cleaners' establishments.

An old lampshade frame covered with plastic can also be used as a cloche, but plastic ones do not usually last very long. It is much better to go to a little more trouble and use glass. Rows of equal-sized glass cloches look very neat in the garden and cannot normally be dislodged by wind and storm. Neither can they be pecked by birds or chewed through by slugs!

The lampshade cloche can, however, make a satisfactory temporary shelter for an up-and-coming new rhubarb plant or other individual plant until it is well-established. Look for old lampshades at jumble sales – where, too, you can frequently find picture frames with glass to make the more permanent cloches.

A small 'cloche' for individual seedlings can be improvised by putting an empty glass jam jar over each seedling.

Jam jars laid on their sides are also very useful to protect ripening strawberries from the attentions of birds, and also will have the effect of cloches as the glass concentrates the sun's rays and thus ripens the strawberries more quickly. If the fruit is ripe, the glass jar will keep it clean until it is ready for picking.

Glass jars are a very useful standby for the gardener, having many such uses. Save all the ones you can spare from jam-making, preserving, bottling, and storage of dry ingredients in the kitchen, especially the smaller ones which are less useful in the kitchen for these purposes (except at jam-making time for putting up free samples for all your friends!)

Pesticides

Here is another area of gardening in which you can make really substantial savings, because you need never buy commercial pesticides (which are usually based on toxic chemicals and should not be used at all by anyone who practises organic gardening, especially on or near food crops).

Ants can be destroyed by pouring boiling water into their nest, though not everyone has an anthill at the bottom of the garden! Soak a sponge in water, wring out, sprinkle with sugar and put it in a dish in the ants' territory. Quite soon it will be full of ants, which can be instantaneously and humanely destroyed by plunging the sponge into boiling water. Coffee grounds are said to destroy them, but I have not tried this method.

Two herbal pesticides which you can make yourself are both particularly effective against aphids (greenfly). One is a herbal 'tea' prepared by pouring two pints of boiling water over two handsful (wearing rubber gloves!) of stinging nettles. If you prefer you can use basil, or four crushed cloves of garlic, instead of nettles. The other pesticidal solution is made by boiling a pound of rhubarb leaves (or elder leaves) for half an hour in a pint of water. These two solutions really do work – the old cottagers of Cobbett's day did know a thing or two! Dilute the concentrated solutions with two pints of tepid water before spraying the aphid-infested plants.

Slugs are the bane of every gardener and a ruthless war must be waged against them if you are not to go out into the garden one morning and see all your young seedlings destroyed. Slugs make their depredations at night, so the measures taken to destroy them must be carried out in the evening. Don't waste money on metaldehyde tablets and other poisonous chemical slug destroyers. Many do not work very effectively anyway. I remember years ago buying a product bearing the legend 'Certain Death to Slugs', which I used as directed. The next day I found twice as many slugs as there had been before using it!

Slugs are for some reason greatly attracted to empty grapefruit halves placed cut side downwards on the soil. In the morning these will be found to contain many of the creatures, which can be destroyed by sprinkling them with salt. Another method is to bury a jam jar up to the neck in the soil near the plants which are at risk from slugs, and pour a little beer into the bottom of the jar. Slugs will make a bee-line (if that is the right word) for this irresistible trap, fall into the jar and drown in the beer. What a way to go!

Snails can be trapped by spreading bran on the surface of the soil and covering it with the discarded outside leaves of cabbage. Don't destroy them but let them go in some place where they will not harm your garden plants. They do quite a lot of good by eating weeds, but have no place in a cultivated garden because they frequently mistake your newly-planted vegetables for groundsel or dock.

Frustrating slugs and snails is another good way to combat the problem, especially if you don't like killing them (or dropping them over next door). Collect the aluminium foil tops from milk bottles, and when transplanting young and vulnerable seedlings cut a hole in the centre of each bottle-top, reverse it and slip the root of the seedling through, then press into the soil. The foil not only tends to retain heat around the roots of the plant and thus encourage more rapid growth, but its sharp edges discourage slugs.

Snipping plastic squeezy bottles into rings is another preventative measure. After cutting off the top and bottom, the average-size bottle will provide you with four rings. Push each ring into the soil around each seedling, and cover with earth so that the top of the ring does not show above the surface. As these plastic rings are smooth, they effectively prevent slugs from getting at the plants as they cannot climb the slippery surface of the plastic. The rings can be re-used indefinitely as they are indestructible.

Weedkillers and fungicides
Salt is a very good weedkiller and can be sprinkled over weeds which grow in the cracks between crazy paving stones, on walls and paths, and similar situations, but it must not be used near the plants you are cultivating. If preferred, a solution of boiling salted water can be poured on instead. This method will clear paths of weeds almost overnight.

Proprietary fungicides to prevent mildew in rose trees are costly and unnecessary. All you need is a handful of ordinary washing soda dissolved in boiling water and left to cool. This is then sprayed over the rose bushes in spring, and does a perfect job. Do not use it when the roses are in bud, or blooming.

A number of weeds need not be destroyed as they have culinary uses. Many, such as dandelion, fat hen, Good King Henry, chickweed, etc. can be used raw in salads or cooked like spinach. It is important to be able to identify the plants correctly. A good book for this purpose is essential. Eat the weeds! Many are rich sources of minerals and vitamins. Besides doing you good, they are a free source of food, and will save you the trouble of destroying them in your garden.

Saving your own seeds
You can save the considerable cost of buying packeted seeds by saving your own seeds in the garden. Beans and peas are left to dry in the pod; other kinds can be gathered when

ready, or paper bags can be tied over the seeding heads to catch any that fall out.

You can also save the seeds from peppers, cucumbers, marrows, courgettes, aubergines, etc. (before cooking, of course). Leave them in a well-ventilated place to dry before sowing. Pips from citrus fruits also grow into attractive houseplants if sown in compost and kept warm. They cannot be grown out of doors. Keep a few potatoes for planting to produce your next year's crop. There is no need at all to purchase seed potatoes for this purpose. Just make sure that the ones you plant are undamaged and absolutely sound, free from any sign of mould or rot. Leave them in a warm place to sprout for about two or three weeks before planting in the garden.

You can also save on the cost of new plants by swapping cuttings of perennials, ornamental shrubs, etc. with friends and neighbours. You can also grow new pot plants suitable for Christmas and birthday presents from cuttings. Fuchsias, geraniums, etc. are easy to grow in this way. By taking cuttings in the spring many of the plants will be ready for Christmas; others do better as cuttings in the autumn and these can be used for birthday presents the following year. You can also save a good deal of money by growing your own houseplants from seed, though you must in this case be prepared to wait sometimes several years for the plant to grow to a reasonable size. However, you will have the satisfaction of growing it yourself. Not all species, however, take so long to mature. Quick growers include tradescantia, kangaroo vine, the ivies, spider plant, and many of the bromeliads (which are not nearly as difficult as they look). Bromeliads may also be propagated from offshoots as well as grown from seed. They make spectacular houseplants and consequently much-appreciated presents.

If you are given carnations, never fail to cut off side shoots and plant them as they are one of the easiest plants to propagate in this way. Dip the end of the side shoot into rooting hormone powder and plant in good compost. You will be rewarded with beautiful carnation plants, each bearing several blooms.

Gladiolus corms and dahlia tubers are often lost by damage from frost. Make a storage box with its own built-in insulation to avoid this waste and consequent expense of replacement. Any box will do – wooden or stout cardboard, it matters little. The secret is to line the box with aluminium foil, which keep the corms and tubers warm and frost-free.

Another use for egg-boxes
This time it's the plastic or styrofoam kind we're talking about (although the papier mâché ones could be used but will take longer to do the job). The job I'm talking of here is ripening green tomatoes. Remove these from the trusses when they are big enough and place in the egg-boxes, one in each section. The tomatoes must not be *too* big as you must be able to close the top of the box. In two days (using plastic or styrofoam boxes) the tomatoes will be ripe. You do not need to place the boxes in a specially warm place – just in normal room temperature.

Storage for onions and garlic
Old tights and nylon stockings make excellent storage containers for onions (and shallots) and garlic. Just drop the bulbs in and hang up the stockings or tights in a well-ventilated dry place, and pull them out as you need them.

Preservative for fences
Creosote is good but it costs money. Make your own outdoor wood preservative for fences and other wooden structures in the garden by mixing equal quantities of paraffin and used engine sump oil from the car.

Floral decorations
If you need green sprays or foliage to put with flowers in a floral arrangement indoors, don't spend money for these at the florist's but grow your own. Laurel, rhododendron, privet, ivy, etc. all make interesting foliage for this purpose and attractive garden shrubs at the same time. If you need ferns for use with indoor flower arrangements,

grow them yourself from spores, in a damp and shady part of your garden.

Save the dead flowerheads of hydrangeas and hang them up to dry. Then spray them with gold or silver paint. They then make attractive and unusual winter floral decorations. Beech leaves should be collected in autumn when at their most brilliant copper hue. Cut some twigs, stand them in a jar containing a mixture of half water and half glycerine, and when the liquid has been absorbed the twigs are ready for arrangement in a dry vase. These very attractive decorations will last all winter and look especially good arranged with everlasting flowers which are easily grown from seed in your garden. You do not need to fill the jar with the water and glycerine mixture – just pour in enough to ensure that the ends of the twigs are immersed. Since the final arrangement requires no water in the vase, that will be one less water-filled pot for the kids to knock over on your best rug.

Honesty should be gathered in autumn when the seed pods have turned white. If honesty does not grow wild in your area you can grow it in the garden. Carefully peel the outer layer from each side of the pod so as to leave only the translucent silvery centre layer. The Chinese lantern plant also makes a beautiful winter decoration when dried. Teasels, grasses and flowering reeds can also be gathered for use in winter floral arrangements. Hang them upside down to dry in a well-ventilated place. No further treatment is needed. Many people spray these with various paints, but I think they look much nicer when left in their natural state.

The garden pond
If you want a small garden pond, recycle an old unwanted kitchen sink. Paint it a more neutral shade to blend in with the colours of the surrounding soil, rocks and plants, but be sure to use only a lead-free paint, or you will kill any plants and fish you introduce after you have sunk it into the ground.

Don't forget to put in the plug!

Finally . . .
Sometimes making a small cash investment results in savings or profits out of all proportion to the amount of your outlay. Therefore – GET THIS BOOK!

Index